FETISH FACTS

Paul Scott

Virgin
BOOKS

First published in 2004 by
Virgin Books
Thames Wharf Studios
Rainville Road
London W6 9HA

A catalogue record for this book is available from the
British Library

ISBN 0 7535 0995 4

Typeset by Phoenix Photosetting, Chatham, Kent
Printed and bound in Great Britain by
Bookmarque Ltd

CONTENTS

CONTENTS

BIOG AND ACKNOWLEDGEMENTS

Paul Scott edits erotica. His previous books include *Saturnalia: a Collection of Bizarre Erotica* and *My Secret Garden Shed: True-Life Male Sexual Fantasies*.

Thanks to: Miss Sharp for Patience and informed contributions to the text, Squaddie John for the Lawrence chat.

INTRODUCTION – WHAT IS FETISHISM?

'In art, only the bizarre is beautiful.' Baudelaire

During the late 1970s, there was a psychology textbook in my school library whose first chapter was headed 'Sexual Perversion'. It featured a black and white picture of some bondage and discipline equipment, the materials laid out flat, cold and calculated to look as unerotic as possible; no one was modelling them. Even so, the picture drew excited chatter from my fellow pupils. There was a hood, some assorted masks, a few leather and rubber tunics and chaps, a flogger, some crops, leg-spreaders and cuffs. Maybe I've embellished the memory with hindsight, but I think I can even remember it all having 1970s styling similar to Lagerfeld's costumes for the movie *Maîtresse*.

I suspect this tableau had been laid out deliberately clinically, like a police exhibit or a murder weapon, as if no one like anyone who could be reading that book would wear it. It was for those to whom pejorative labels could be applied, making them 'other'. Presentation is everything. Of course, this only made the items more appealing, mysterious, forbidden and transgressive. Put these on, the book seemed to say, and you put on the label 'kinky' in the same instant. Ooh, the shame!

It seemed to me that the clinical psychologists who wrote the book were like nineteenth-century botanists – they had pottered off on a voyage to categorise every known plant, including the more exotic varieties, trying to understand something larger than themselves. If they did not grasp the biology at first glance, they at least flagged and labelled everything so they could return later with the proper tools of understanding. Reasonable enough, but sexual facts seemed to be included in that textbook like imperial plunder, grabbed and thrown in the hold: they hadn't yet become knowledge. They'd been taxonomically catalogued, but were not as understood as was claimed.

The fact that these items were in a book about behaviour that wasn't 'normal' didn't seem consistent with the fact that most of my pubertal peers had joined the throng around the picture, expressing at least a prurient interest. And the twenty-something years between then and now have only confirmed that impression, as fetish style has become mainstream. That book pretended to understand its subject, and had the dry air of academic authority, while not offering any insights or resonances beyond attaching labels to behaviours. It gave no sense of their reality, except as things inconceivable, strange and intriguing. It could only be read pruriently – it was 'fact-sploitation', and it didn't respect the experiences of its subjects.

I hope this book does the opposite and leaves room for a bit of intuited understanding of fetishism as a creative process. Long may fetish and its inspirational wellsprings remain barely conceived, strange and intriguing, as anything must that is to evolve.

On the Conveyor Belt Tonight

So what is fetish? This book looks at a style phenomenon that's about sex, but is something different to sexual explicitness – or, rather, it may or may not be explicit, but doesn't make the bland assumption that explicitness by itself is arousing. This book is not about fetishism as part of sex play. What you won't find here is a list of the lip-smackin', thirst-quenchin' things fetishists do. There are as many differences between people as there are people, and there'll be exceptions to any generalisation. To be part of fetish style, however, we must celebrate, or at least refer to, fetishistic behaviour.

Doctor Freud

As Freud described it in 1887, sexual fetishes are a result of castration anxiety, and therefore only men can be fetishists. His theory is unscientific, and dependent on the specifics of patriarchal Viennese society in his day. In time, castration anxiety has gone the way of penis envy, but Freud did identify the link between human orgasms and conditioning, which remains true. Fetish therefore is often about *stuff*, although one can similarly eroticise an experience or sensation too. Whether we think we know why or not, there will be some individual things that each of us finds arousing in a fetishistic way. It could be the wearing of glasses (a popular one); it could be a specific texture or fabric that is irresistible to our touch; it could be the sight of a woman teetering in high heels, calf muscles taut – anything that could be part of a private, self-determined if occasionally surprising pattern of arousal. We are all fetishists but, for many, the everyday nature of their fetishes means they do not have to think of themselves as such.

Freud's assumption was that since sexual perversion was so *outré*, those indulging in it must be acting through compulsion rather than desire – a circular argument, but one that persists. Any explanation of fetishism usually begins with a tiresome reference to the fetish-objects of African peoples for whom the idol itself was thought to be the godhead, or at least something in which the worshipped spirit inhered. The presence of the object itself was necessary for worship to take place. Because of his assumption that the presence of the sexual fetish-object was necessary for a true sexual fetishist to become satisfyingly aroused, Freud borrowed the word 'fetish' for the arousing object or material in an anthropologically colonialist way, describing both African peoples and kinky people in reductive terms.

Basques and Separatists

While it's true that some self-identified perverts would say quite happily that they couldn't get aroused except during sex of their chosen flavour, then that's also because they choose not to. Where it remains an assumption that fetishists actually require the presence of their fetish for arousal, it is easy to retain an idea of sexual perversity as a marginal activity. There will always be separatist perverts, drawn to the idea of lifestyle SM relationships, sometimes on a contractual basis, that extend into every area of their lives. Occasionally these perverts, while requesting understanding and respect for themselves, disdain other people's entry-level kinky fun, or switching, as polluting the pure sensibility of their self-proclaimed 'it's cool to be an outsider' marginality. As if we don't all start somewhere.

For these people, the idea of being thought of as normal is a nightmare. But they are self-identified. It's not the business of clinical medicine, religion or the law to describe people that way unless they really are unhappy paraphiliacs in need of help. Meanwhile, the assumption that kinky people need the presence of their fetish object for arousal – and probably hate themselves afterwards – serves to obscure the fact that they are generally no more or less in control of their sexuality than anyone else, and obscure just how mainstream fetish style is.

Sub-Culture

If fetishism can be about material things, then it's specific to time and place: many costumes at eighteenth-century masquerades drew on history and myth for their inspiration, and some costumes in a fetish club today have been inspired by masquerades. The eroticism of particular materials is similarly specific to time and place. One culture's prosaic everyday detail – such as warming, practical animal furs – becomes another culture's exotic attraction. This isn't just true of sex, but it's as true of sex as of anything else. Different times and places can seem magical and evocative to us, despite being full, at the time, of people who found the reality prosaic, dull or just plain adverse. If it's true that we sexualise our fears, and that human sexuality can be a coping mechanism, then perhaps fetishistic sex helps us to accept our mortal human lot.

Fetishism is inextricably linked with one's mortality when it's a celebration of materials that are limited to time and place.

In consensual SM, the top is sometimes characterised as the instrument of the bottom's desire to punish themselves, and the bottom as applying *self*-discipline with the aid of the top. Kinky sex is therefore the triumph of the submissive's will. On this view, sub-dom relationships are triangulated relationships with oneself, just as for a religious devotee in a mediaeval convent the whipper is merely the instrument of God's will, a catalyst. There's some truth in this, but the idea that pervs are necessarily unhappy people now seems profoundly dated. The fact that fetishism is conditioned behaviour does not mean it's beyond an individual's control. You want to explore more of a powerful experience, not repeat it, as early psychoanalysts believed. Like its close relative, horror, fetish is the perishable fruit of the unconscious and the imagination. It's not about breaking laws. It's not about confounding anyone else's choices. The *real*, meaningful boundaries one transgresses are personal rather than social. Beliefs do not exist in opposition to each other – a shaman can be a clinical psychologist and vice versa. By entering a playful kinky zone, with all its accoutrements and materials, fetishists can get a lot of fun from becoming something other than what they have to be 90 per cent of the time. It is no scarier than adults playing dressing-up games. Meanwhile, the idea that pervs are trapped in a psychotherapeutic dead-end ignores the redemptive value of an ample sense of humour. In many animals, fighting and mating is indistinguishable. Sexual abnormality? Sex is pretty irrational in itself.

1: THE TIME MACHINE – FETISHISM THROUGH HISTORY

Imagine you're at a fetish gathering. Taxis have arrived, setting down office workers, probation officers, advertising executives, mechanics, estate agents – some already fancying themselves as denizens of the night. Others are in the cloakroom, balancing first on one foot and then the other, peeling and zipping themselves into second skins, in a flurry of talcum powder.

Apart from the surly bar staff in their regulation T-shirts – the only *real* uniforms on display all evening – everyone has affected a transformation. Who, or what, do you see around you? Those who ordinarily feel mousy are strutting around, straight-backed in a peacock pose. There's an army officer dressed as a chauffeur, a driver dressed as a soldier. A doctor dresses as a schoolgirl while a teacher dresses as a nurse. A bibbed and nappied adult baby sulks as his TV nurse play-whips him; a drag-king sailor with tattooed anchors and a goatee gets a hug from a petite Madam Butterfly in a kimono. A woman in little but a leather harness flashes her tits and whinnies coltishly. A burlesque starlet with a feather boa is cornered by a sermon from a pervy priest. Here and there, near-naked men kneel like expectant puppies.

Of course, there's no legislating for *real* originality. Even so, what are some of the major influences from history on this circus-parade of people? From where on Earth, whether they know it or not, have they drawn their inspiration? And from how long ago?

WHEN THE SAINTS GO MARCHING IN ...

The history of the Christian church still continues to provide a source for fetish imagery even as, in the UK especially, the role of the traditionally robed, dog-collared sacerdotal type is in decline. Where Christianity thrives these days, it's the smart-but-casual world of Evangelism. Writers from André de Nerciat to Georges

Bataille continued a robust European tradition of anti-clerical writing that mixed the erotic and shocking, and today we have the art of Andres Serrano and rubber nuns and priests in fetish clubs. The reason's simple – ecclesiastical matters make for great role play. The more we become a nation of spiritually wishy-washy agnostics at one remove from the real thing, the more the hellfire preacher becomes a caricature ripe for parody.

Rules within Rules

It's not that long ago that many Europeans and Americans felt the routine impact of organised faith in their lives – whether the infamously treated 'Magdalene Sisters' of 1960s Ireland, the Pentecostal brethren of *Oranges Are Not the Only Fruit* or the millions who were simply more socially obliged to attend church services, or go through benign rights of passage of baptism and confirmation, than we are today. People not only followed the law of the land but ecclesiastical orthodoxy into the bargain. One might not have got arrested for working on the Sabbath – at least not in this life – but one still didn't do it.

Anything that offers rules within rules is bound to resonate with pervs, who love to fetishise closed communities: from the monastery in Sade's *The Misfortunes of Virtue* to the real-life femdom holiday resort, The Other World Kingdom, based in the Czech Republic. Rules that you can break are the first requirement of any game, and so religion is a game to the faithless. If it doesn't cost you anything to submit, to confirm or to deny a faith when you want a game to stop, then those who really do die or endure pain for their faith might hold a fascination for you.

Forgive Me, Father

Add celibacy to that and you've a sexual tension that's right up the street of anyone who gets off on the *idea* of sex as much as sex itself. Once upon a time, the Roman Catholic Church provided a large number of both men and women with a role in life: close quartering, ritual interaction and a belief in something that could be corrupted by rewarding sexual desire. And just because your sexual tension is natural, that doesn't mean you shouldn't attempt to scourge it from yourself as the product of original sin, in which context 'natural' is bad, a siren-song sent to try us. Funny how that physical self-abnegation, that triumph of the mind over the body, provides its own relief. The Lord moves in mysterious ways, his wonders to perform ...

To cut through the papal bull, here are the stories of the top seven potentially pervy saints, in no particular order. There are two aspects to their sainthood: suffering, death and physical torture, but also – for St Catherine, as for many others including St Theresa – the heights of sexual epiphany and mystical union with her Messiah, thanks in part to the suppression of her actual sensual self. This crosses over strongly with fetishistic pleasure too: what perv doesn't also believe that their kinky predilection will lead to a far more deeply rewarding, endorphin-fuelled experience than what John Lydon famously described as 'two-minutes and fifty-four seconds of squelching noises'?

Celebrity Sainthood

This heady mix of fearful aspiration illustrates how the lives of the saints were and are living cultural stories to Catholics. It is glib but informative to say that they fulfilled a role similar to celebrities within the early mediaeval and Renaissance Church: as role-models, figures to identify with and talking points. Christianity has been more secularised, sexualised and worldly than we're inclined to think in these waning days of vestigial state spirituality. When we think of sex and religion, perverts and pedagogues, we think of unworldly vicars or naughty nuns – comic figures for playful games, and perhaps a little whiff of candle-smoke, a bit of the pentacled, tentacled or satanic. In other words, we think of SM and fetish as borrowing the language of religion and pastiching it. If religion used to have more secular and social relevance than it does today, then people may bring the same impulses of faith and self-identification that they might once have brought to church to other pursuits like sexual perversion. In so far as a religion is that which informs your thoughts, however irregularly observed, and something you might stick up for to your own embarrassment in a pub conversation, then perverts are religious.

Add to this the role of ritual – as opposed to scripture – in religion, and it seems there are further pervy parallels. Roman Catholicism especially is a sacramental tradition, and knowing the Old Testament and Gospels is not in itself the act of faith it is for Protestants. In addition to the sacrament there are the reveries of St Theresa or St Jerome. Altered states that were once matters of belief are still likely to be matters of ritual, and a ritual can be anything that makes you aware of what you are doing and trying to achieve. To have a fetish wedding, for example, is both to miss and make the point that weddings are fetishistic anyway, while you don't have to be a saint to know that stimulating the body can alter the mind.

Saint Catherine of Alexandria (fetishes: chastity, sadism)
The story of Catherine of Alexandria is told in *The Golden Legend* (see below). She was a Christian convert of noble birth who, as a young woman, had a vision, or sensual reverie, in which she 'married' Christ. The Roman Emperor Maxentius took a shine to her and tried to persuade her to abandon her faith. When he failed, he sent a phalanx of fifty philosophers to have a go, but she converted them to Christianity by the force of her argument.

A possessive sort, Maxentius had the philosophers executed and imprisoned Catherine, who then converted his wife and two hundred of his soldiers. After killing them, Maxentius had Catherine strapped down for torture to death upon the wheel. (It's from the wheel's appearance in the lives of the saints that it became a common mediaeval European punishment.) The wheel, however, was destroyed by a miraculous thunderbolt, and Catherine was beheaded instead with a sword. This reflects a Dark Age and mediaeval view of punishment: although it may not seem so to us because of her death, her story is redemptive in that she died without the excess of torture that was considered appropriate for 'justice' to be done. Her quick death, for those who knew the lives of the saints, was a studio ending, as much as if she'd leapt off the wheel into a hero's arms.

St Catherine's was one of the voices heard by Joan of Arc – another bride of Christ – and it's after her that the Catherine Wheel is named.

Saint Joan of Arc (fetishes: chastity, genderplay)

In her short life (1412–1431), Jeanne d'Arc led the French to victory against the English and was executed for her pains. She was born of peasants in Lorraine during the One Hundred Years' War, slap-bang in the middle of the turbulence of this conflict of succession. The French crown had passed to Henry VI of England by treaty after the bloody Battle of Agincourt, and the English occupied northern France. But the French nobility refused to acquiesce, and backed the rightful claim of the Dauphin Charles, son of Charles VI.

Joan claimed to hear the voices of St Michael the Archangel, St Catherine and St Margaret telling her to free France and install the Dauphin on the throne. At sixteen she asked to join his forces but was rejected. Returning the following year in a man's battle clothes, she was allowed to meet the Dauphin. After having her interrogated by Church authorities, he agreed to her plan of relieving Orleans, which was under siege from the English.

With her brothers by her side, clad in armour and with a white *fleur-de-lis* banner, she re-energised French fighters with her piety and confidence, and the siege was raised. By the end of her campaign as the Maid of Orleans, Charles was crowned king at Reims.

In an effort to liberate another town, Compeigne, Joan was captured by the Burgundians. She tried to escape twice (the second time by jumping from a tall tower) and was eventually sold to the Bishop of Beauvais who was allied with the English.

She was accused of heresy in 1431. Her insistence that she communicated directly with God through voices was interpreted as disobedience to the Church. Her 'suicide attempt' of jumping from the tower, as well as her cross-dressing, was also cited in the trial. She claimed never to have killed anybody; to have only carried the standard during battles. She was made to promise to stop dressing as a man. Against the standard rules of process, she was kept in a prison guarded by English soldiers, instead of the bishopric prison. Possibly to protect herself, she dressed again as a man. Hence she was considered to have fallen again into sin.

When she was shown the torture instruments, she said that she intended to simply retract afterwards everything she would admit under torture. Her judges decided against torturing her. After the University of Paris confirmed her guilt, she was convicted and turned over to the secular arm for execution.

While burning to death at Rouen, she repeatedly shouted the name of Jesus. After she had died, the flames were put out and her partly cooked body was shown to the crowd, in order to prove that she was indeed a woman. Then she was completely burned. Heretics at the time could not receive a Christian burial, and Joan's remains were cast into the river Seine.

Joan's sin was not to be a military leader in enemy hands but to annoy the Church authority by claiming a visionary hotline to God's will. After Charles gained Rouen, a second trial resulted in the nullification of her conviction, although she was not canonised until 1920. Joan's legend has its dark side – the notorious occultist and child-killer Gilles de Rais, himself burnt at the stake, had served with her.

Saint Jerome (fetish: masochism)

A second-century scholar, Jerome translated the Bible *into* Latin (that's how early a Christian he was), and was an advisor to one of the first Popes. He's the one who is said to have removed a thorn from a lion's paw as an act of faith. What he did, however, was shrive himself routinely in the desert, using the subjection of his body to achieve the Nirvanic, altered state of mind that a modern primitive such as Fakir Musafar might describe as 'sub-space'. It's a perfectly legitimate lifestyle choice.

Mary Magdalene (fetishes: love, feet)

Mary Magdalene came to Christ as a penitent 'fallen' woman. She washed his feet with her tears, and dried them with her hair. According to Luke's Gospel, Mary was exorcised of seven devils by Christ – powerful stuff: does one orgasm as a demon leaves the body? Present at the Crucifixion, she was the first person to whom the resurrected Christ is said to have appeared, with the words 'touch me not', his intention being to show that she and his followers should feel his comfort whether or not he was around. That's men for you.

It's pretty literal-minded to start describing these Gospel stories as examples of particular sexual fetishes. But the point is that in the monocultural days of the Dark Ages and the mediaeval period, the Church, as the sole source of culture, informed its followers' sexual imaginations too. In that sense, the lives of the saints were its pornography. If you were to access foot-fetish material today, Mary's cathartic supplication, shame, abasement and self-abnegation might be just what you craved. And in a fetishistic context you too might find a perverse comfort in being denied your lover's touch.

Saint Sebastian (fetishes: bondage, sadism)

Saint Sebastian served as a captain in Rome's Praetorian Guard, a dashing figure in the city and a hit with the ladies. He was also a secret Christian convert who used his position to lessen the privations of imprisoned Christians. For this, he was sentenced to death by Emperor Diocletian.

Tied to a tree (or, in an alternative version, a column), his arms above his head to expose his chest, or seated languidly in later Renaissance versions, he was shot by his own archers. He survived the arrows, which miraculously failed to pierce any vital organ, and in some versions was nursed to health by a local widow. Eventually he was stoned or clubbed to death, and his body thrown into a sewer.

The attempt to make his own reluctant men kill him was an authoritarian mind-game that didn't work: like Christ, he rose again. Like Spartacus, he's a political figure who's been sexualised, a symbol of brotherhood, tenderness and cruelty. In Yukio Mishima's *Confessions of a Mask,* the narrator describes his first boyhood ejaculation to Reni's portrait of Sebastian, and pictures of the saint, all corded sinew and knotted cord, are legion, not least in Derek Jarman's elegiac eponymous portrait of 1982.

Saint Simon Stylites (fetishes: abstinence, purity)

Simon Stylites began his working life as a shepherd boy for his father's flock in northern Syria in the fifth century. When he was just thirteen he heard the Gospel passage 'Blessed are they that mourn; blessed are the clean of heart.' An old man then told him that eternal happiness could only be achieved with suffering, and that solitude was the surest way to attain it. Impressed by this explanation, the young Simon joined the hermits in a nearby monastery.

He tried out a number of different monasteries, but seems to have found them far too convivial, and determined to go one better in the denial of worldly goods by taking his place on the top of a tall pillar. Like a figure invented by the Monty Python team, Simon remained, most of the time standing – sometimes on one leg – exposed to inclement weather and absorbed in continuous prayer. He died in 459 at the age of 69, having spent 36 years on the top of different pillars. The unrepentantly atheist Spanish film director Luis Buñuel committed Simon's life to surrealistic celluloid in 1965 in *Simon of the Desert*. The film speculates gleefully on the sexual torments Simon may have endured: a young blonde temptress in a sailor's costume, black stockings and pigtails plays hoopla around his plinth; a deformed goatherd insinuates one of his flock may offer him some 'personal' company, with the warning, 'the devil lives in the desert', and so on. Buñuel's 45-minute dry take on the absurdity of extreme asceticism and the denial of pleasure sums up the pointlessness of deferring gratification.

John the Baptist

Honourable mention also goes to St John the Baptist, for the appearance of Salome. John was the prophet who preached the coming of the Messiah, and was Christ's second cousin. He set up his stall in the desert, baptising followers in the Jordan river. In the pivotal moment of his life, he recognised Jesus as the Messiah when he came to be baptised. John made an enemy of King Herod by criticising him for taking his half-brother's wife as his queen, and was imprisoned. Queen Herodias' daughter Salome danced for Herod so lewdly that he fatefully granted her the lurid wish her mother had put her up to, and presented her with John's head on a salver. Salome was the original, and literal, *femme fatale*, whose blithe decadence caused Herod to lose his head, and John his. She inspired Caravaggio, Moreau, Beardsley and Wilde.

The Golden Legend

Many lives of the saints are recorded in *The Golden Legend*, written in the late thirteenth century by a Dominican friar who went on to become archbishop of Genoa. Full of tension and release, religious punishment and ritual redemption, the lives of the saints chronicle sexual denial and hands-off epiphanies similar to Courtly Love, another forerunner of fetish, while other saints were martyrs to lurid sexual rapaciousness. Their suffering was something to aspire to, as seen in the routine martyrdoms of the religious wars of Europe.

The Lives of the Saints

Saints were not only fearful but also aspirational figures; their suffering was noble and their martyrdom an ultimate achievement. One can see something of this in the way particular saints have been patrons of specific sufferings. There was succour for the distressed Christian in not only praying to but identifying with the saint whose sufferings your own were, in their more prosaic way, most similar to – for example:

- St Stephen's stoning was witnessed by St Paul, and his patronage extends to those who suffer from headaches.

- St Appollonia was a deaconess in Alexandria, who, threatened with immolation, jumped into the fire herself. Her teeth had been broken as she was tortured to renounce her faith, and she is the patron saint of dentists.

- St Barbara, who is the patron saint of builders and protects against artillery, was locked in a tower by her own father but escaped. When he had killed her, he was struck by lightning.

- The name of St Sebastian was invoked against plague, since bubonic boils were thought to resemble the arrow punctures in his flesh, and the shots of archers to be as random as the progress of the disease.

- St Agatha could have avoided punishment by sleeping with her captors, but preferred to keep her fidelity to Christ. When she refused to work in a brothel, her breasts were cut off in a sexually motivated martyrdom. In recent times her help has been sought by women suffering from breast cancer.

You Gotta Serve Somebody

Scourges, fasting and hair shirts were *de rigueur* for a certain model of sainthood.

- St Angela of Foligno drank water contaminated by the putrefying flesh of a leper.

- St Margaret of Cortona had to be dissuaded from despoiling her facial beauty with a razor.

- St Maria Maddalena dei Pazzi lay naked on thorns.

- Catherine of Siena drank pus from a cancerous sore.

- A confessor ordered Veronica Giuliani to clean the walls and floor of her cell with her tongue, a command she proudly exceeded by swallowing the spiders and their webs too.

Holy Anorexics

Arachnids aside, starvation was a constant, and these saints compelled their bodies to wither away, not only through ritual fasting but through what we'd now say were bingeing reactions to it. According to historian Rudolph Bell, they were 'holy anorexics' who, although different from *anorexia nervosa* sufferers, do show that this fatal form of self-harm predated the stick-thin dictates of the fashion industry.

These women who gave their obliging natures to Jesus raise awkward questions: they are relatively modern, but experienced the lurid sufferings of their mediaeval predecessors. Even in pervy terms, their relationship with God just wasn't safe, sane and consensual. Lying naked on thorns? A kind of edge-play you could recover from, but drinking a leper's bathwater is going a bit far, on anyone's health insurance!

But Seriously …

We can think they're silly, and be atheistically satirical, but that doesn't help us to understand their beliefs. They were histrionic perhaps, but considered the payoff worthwhile: that sharing the pain of the cross was fair exchange for their visionary gleam, or else a sacrifice for others. In the context of their faith, their suffering had meaning and could be put to work. Without it, we see only their squalor and their neglect of the physical, and lack the means to see the consent they gave. We may think they were delusional; question whether they really had free will; attribute clinical labels; or at least describe their inner experiences as the products of endorphins and chemicals. We look for ways to dissuade others from similar self-harm.

In the nineteenth and early twentieth centuries – when most of these women were canonised – obscure sexual preferences and modish perversions were likewise described without exception as harmful paraphilias, as was homosexuality, by the medical profession and others lacking the context to understand them. Which is where, for many, the image of religious types as proscriptive, moralistic killjoys comes from. Nonetheless, we'd do well to remember that failure to understand is something of which we can be guilty too.

FIT TO BE TIED: FEUDAL JAPAN

Give 'em Enough Rope

Rope bondage has become a familiar sight in kinky imagery. Every internet user of fetish sites is likely to have been bombarded, at some point, with a series of unstoppable pop-up porn ads, some of which feature Japanese rope bondage. Japanese-American women are in demand as models in the USA by porn producers who want to make their rope bondage look 'authentic'. There's a world of difference between the ad hoc, and possibly dangerous, tying of a lover's wrists, and the elaborate butterfly structures found on the fetish scene and in porn, often designed to flatter and delineate the body in a manner similar to clothing and – thanks to generally using wide iterations of rope to form a band at stress points – comfortable (or at least not painful in the *wrong* way).

Ropes and Knots

Additionally, rope itself can be used to stimulate: there are many different preferences for material, thickness and weave of rope. Most agree that nylon belongs on boats, and while there's an ecologically driven revival in the use of hemp for clothing, in rope bondage it never went away. Knots themselves can also be used – cautiously – at differing pressure and pleasure points. Rope or hide can be used in these ways to form a stimulating harness for the body without necessarily restraining limbs, something associated with modern primitives and Native American rituals.

There are internet discussion groups where you can debate ideal lengths for different patterns. Acolytes of the fetish scene, such as fetish diva Midori, run rope-bondage workshops in clubs, and there's a community for whom it's not foreplay but a main event. So there's a world of difference between the edge of rope-play and the hurried tying of a lover with a length of anything to hand. How did rope bondage become so evolved? We owe the idea of that to the Japanese.

No One Ties 'em Like These Guys

It was known as *Hojo Jutsu* or *Nawa Shibari* in feudal Japan, and was learned by the samurai class, who, in addition to being awesome fighters, were enforcers of the civil law. It evolved first as warfare and was taught as a martial art, by sensei in their schools, or *ryu*, in case a need arose to keep a person alive and take them captive, or prevent their escape. A prisoner may be facing interrogation or else, as was often the case in feudal Japan, be someone of enough importance to an opposing warlord's faction to exchange. Another purpose was to bring a suspect before a magistrate. Throughout the world, it seems, the feudal period was peppered with ways of securing prisoners. No one, however, had evolved as sophisticated a science as the Japanese.

Hold Tight!

Rope bondage was incorporated into the warrior's fighting skills during the bloody *Sengoku Jidai* or 'warring states' period of the sixteenth century and, despite the coveted value of their skills, an abbreviated form of the samurai's *Hojo Jutsu* was later taught to the lower-class police officers, the *okapiki*. The ropes were generally made of tightly wound linen that had been beaten until soft. Hooks were incorporated, allowing someone to be brought down as if with a lariat. Uniquely, they were used as a matter of social manners as well as practical restraint, reinforcing humiliation and giving signals about how to treat a prisoner. The manner in which prisoners were tied denoted both their rank and social status, and the nature of their crimes, in a commonly recognised way. Knots, too, were perfected according to whether they were to tighten or remain fast, and how strong the prisoner was.

The Semiotics of Rope

During the Edo period (1603–1867), the semiotics of rope was further refined to include especially dyed ropes. According to what is known, violet denoted a high-class suspect, black low, white a minor crime and blue a violent crime. These specifics may or may not be correct, but something equivalent certainly evolved. As a form of torture, too, suspects were bound into agonising stress positions. Although rope bondage originated in Japan, we should be skeptical of anyone who invites us home on the basis that their rope bondage techniques are derived from *Hojo Jutsu*. Its details are lost to history, and the idea that anyone's time-consuming *Kinbaku* elaborations today, however skilful, ingenious or beautiful, bear any relation to a grappling, wrestling, fast martial art stretches the imagination.

EIGHTEENTH-CENTURY FRANCE

Pleasure at Any Price

Britain was shocked by the French Revolution. Men of letters such as Edmund Burke wrote in praise of the political status quo, and much of what's conservative about British intellectual culture solidified thereafter, lest something like it happen here. But France hadn't been any nicer during the years of its *ancien régime*, which had spanned most of the eighteenth century. Such routine brutality had remained unremarked-upon because it trickled downwards, from the aristocracy to the poor. Ideas of the Enlightenment, such as the supremacy of law, were not known beyond the Paris salons. A routine judicial punishment was the hideous torture of 'breaking on the wheel', and at such executions the upper classes would copulate behind the drawn blinds of their carriages as they watched the horror unfold.

Until you think that breaking on the wheel was not technically an execution as such, you don't grasp why Dr Guillotine was a humane man. But the executioner's art was to aim his blows at the victim's limbs, pelvic bone and ribs in such a way as to prolong the agony, often with the aid of various restorative draughts and preparations. A man might first have had his genitals wrenched off, and a woman her breasts. Once the wretch's broken limbs were contorted around the wheel and fastened in place so that they could be made to stare directly down at the upturned soles of their feet, they were hoisted aloft on a long pole and left to die as the birds pecked at their eyeballs, still aware as they began their inexorable transition into carrion. Out in the countryside, anything could happen.

The upper-class saying was 'pleasure at any price' – but it was usually the lower orders, not they themselves, who paid the price for their libidinous experimentation. This was a world of rustling silks and satins, of *Liaisons Dangereux*, of extreme libertinage and a society obsessed with sex. It had its lighter side: bookstalls were full of erotic literature. Art during this period was equally fascinated with the human body and sensuality. Fashion and dress had also gone to extremes in exaggerating tight waists, swelling cleavages and elaborate bustles.

Louis XV (1710–1774) is quite possibly the most libidinous monarch of all time – no mean feat. He had an extraordinary number of mistresses, going so far as to have his own private bordellos in his deer park. He cost the treasury purse over one billion *livres*, not even accounting for other enormous expenses such as the care of the extraordinary number of illegitimate children he fathered.

The King even had a specific minister, the *Intendant de Menus-Plaisirs* (the Minister of Dainty Pleasures), whose sole duty it was to organise the King's orgies at the bordellos in the deer park. It is said that these events made any Roman Saturnalia pale by comparison. What the royal court did, the rest of society, fanning out to the provincial nobility, followed. Not even the clergy were exempt from the debauchery of the period. Contemporary Parisian police records show hundreds of arrests of monks, curates and other religious workers caught in acts of indecency.

Bawdy Houses

During the reign of Louis XV, prostitution had enjoyed widespread patronage and toleration in Paris. Many houses were under direct police protection. However, there were laws on the books governing these activities, and there were instances of arrested prostitutes being sent to the penal colony of New Orleans. Even so, it was estimated that there were twenty thousand prostitutes in Paris, with a population of six hundred thousand. Not surprisingly, a full *à la carte* menu of kinky bondage and flagellatory pleasures was available.

The Revolution itself didn't repress this licentiousness but extended it to all classes. It is estimated that the number of prostitutes increased by half again at the onset of revolution in 1789. By 1791, all laws governing paid sex were done away with, and it was held that any restriction would be an affront to personal liberty. A scene that the Marquis de Sade describes in *Juliette*, in which it is recommended that Juliette show herself half naked in the streets to the public if she wants to remove the last vestiges of her modesty, is far from fictional. During Year V of the Revolution, two women paraded up and down the Champs-Elysées, nude except for a thin gauze, in order to rid themselves of such a bourgeois conception. It's easy to think of Sade as disturbed, a lone freak. But in the context of his world, he looks more like a man anxious to portray what he saw as the sexual origins of physical and mental exploitation.

Masked Balls

> *Where sexes blend in one confus'd intrigue*
> *Where idle girls ravish and men grow big*
> Christopher Pitt (*On the Masquerade*, 1727)

Mistaken identity is a common artistic device, from the genderfuck Sapphic titillation of Shakespeare's *As You Like It* to twentieth-century cinema. Identity confusion at a masked ball is a dramatic cliché that came to us from the eighteenth-century novels of Richardson, Smollett, Defoe and Fielding. The real history of eighteenth-century London's masquerades, however, is far more exciting than the mannered events we might imagine, and there wasn't a lot of curtseying and bowing, unless it was ironic. Anonymity – among invited guests – has always been a key to freedom, after all, and eighteenth-century Londoners found getting dressed up to be a signifier for sanctioned misbehaviour as much as revellers did in London's pervy boom years of the 1990s.

Such events could easily be described as 'licentious', deriving from 'licence', which comes from the Latin *licere*, 'to be permitted'. This bit of etymology takes us back to the culture of Saturnalia, the ancient Romans' hedonistic festivals in honour of Saturn: sanctioned chaos in which the social order was turned on its head. The 'Lord of Misrule' who was born therein found his way into the riotous winter festivals of mediaeval England, in which, with the help of nature spirits like The Green Man, benign chaos was encouraged; it was acceptable, for a period, to talk back to your 'betters'; a sense of real upheaval could be flirted with; and people could step out of their usual roles with the knowledge that order would be restored in due course. The upper orders of feudal society perhaps hated it, or perhaps joined in, but either way they must have known that for people without a chance of fulfilling their aspirations, or even of having a concept of them, it was a social safety valve. It was riot, but it was not revolution – and it was a lot to do with keeping warm. An anaemic echo of these festivals is to be heard in the snap of a modern Christmas cracker.

Merrie England

The celebrants of Saturnalia, the revellers of Misrule, the denizens of a masquerade and the diamonds in the rough of clubland are part of a fetishistic tradition of pleasure-taking. In each case, a form of creative chaos ensues, where the ultimate harmlessness of the role-play is understood. These zones of temporary anarchy are 'carnivalesque', and identities are self-consciously played with. Like carnival, these events take over our everyday spaces, from hired-out clubs to the high street. In eighteenth-century London, masquerades took place in public gardens, assembly rooms, theatres and brothels, all decked out for the occasion.

Hogarth satirised the sexuality of masquerades as early as the 1720s. By the 1740s, they were not just invitation-only events but huge public parties, held at locations such as Vauxhall Gardens, Dog and Duck Gardens and Marylebone. In May 1771, according to *Town and Country* magazine, nearly two thousand revellers attended a masquerade at the Pantheon, held at the King's Theatre in London's Haymarket. Masquerade costume-shops flourished for around thirty years. Popular costumes broke taboos, and drew on classical myth, Shakespeare and the fashionably orientalist *Arabian Nights*. All manner of pervy ecclesiastical types would be present, from periwigged drag kings and queens to tits-out classical Dianas with bows and arrows. Judy might be beating Mr Punch; Adam and Eve, fig-leaves in place, would be carousing with cardinals and popes while flirtatious fauns and obliging tavern wenches clinched with lusty soldiers and horny demons.

All-night Revelry

Masquerades were all-nighters: the revels kicked off around 10 p.m. and the drinking, dancing and intrigue continued into the next day. At the posh end, Teresa Cornelys, opera singer and friend of Casanova, held famous parties at Carlisle House in Soho Square in the 1760s, while John James Heidegger, known as 'the Count', the first and best-remembered face on the scene, had hosted weekly balls from the 1720s until his death in 1749; they were held at The Haymarket, and up to a thousand guests were present. Despite and because of their *beau monde* image, they were a subversive mix of class and gender to which today's fetish clubs, such as Torture Garden, aspire: ticket prices aside, 'all state and ceremony are laid aside since the peer and the Apprentice, the Punk [working girl] and the Duchess are upon equal foot,' reported the *Weekly Journal* in the 1750s. What could be more sub-dom? There was even a genre of 'masque-sploitation' litera-ture in which salacious tales of falls from grace thanks to mistaken identity or drunkenness were woven into lurid plots, in prose full of opprobrium but sparing no explicit details, such as *Masquerade; or, the Devil's Nursery* (1732) and *The Female Spectator* (1746).

From Caliban to the Taliban

One influence on the masquerade was the exoticism of mainland Europe. Young aristocrats had returned from the Grand Tour with a cosmopolitan veneer and bawdy tales of the bacchanals of Venice; Italian and French styles were in the ascendant. Time was called on the fun, sadly, by Britain's conservative response to the French Revolution of 1789. People were understandably less inclined to fantasise and flirt with transgression when the terrible fruits of real chaos were being seen and heard in periodicals and from the lips of the aristocracy's frightened *émigré* friends. Londoners, after all, were only partying for its own sake, not partying for their right to fight. French and English ideologues with their literal notions of liberty stomped on the flickerings of genuinely playful freedoms, only to become Cromwells in their turn.

The style of masquerades, however, continued to influence a legion of designers, artists and clubbers from Vivienne Westwood OBE to the New Romantics. Although Byron wrote of attending a masquerade at Burlington House in 1814, they had by then pretty much become more sanitised affairs, evolving eventually into our desexualised fancy-dress parties. Similarly, the hedonism and sensation-seeking of the 1990s have given way to realism and terror, as they did in the 1790s. Meanwhile the Lord of Misrule is biding his time, Caliban-like, watching our clash of fundamentalisms and waiting to pounce.

THE ENGLISH VICE

Corporal Punishment and Flagellant Fantasies

We're used to thinking of the Victorians as seething repositories of sexual repression who beat each other as frequently as we shake hands, yet never acknowledged the arousal it caused. Lazily, we repeat the half-truth that the Victorians were made apoplectic by the sight of a naked ankle, and kept their dining-table legs covered out of the same sense of propriety. In this view, the history of corporal punishment in Great Britain is a thought-provoking example of social relativism, in which things once not considered sexual now are.

In fact, however, it's debatable that the Victorians were at all unaware of the arousing function of corporal punishment. Individuals may have been naïve, but flagellants spoke to each other in subtextual, ritualised, codified ways that have since been misinterpreted as the very straight-lacedness that wanted flesh covered up. They were not all that different from us. The Victorians knew what they were doing. It was accepted by many, and shockingly to us, that a sexual element in a forced corporal punishment (CP) situation was sometimes simply an all-well-and-good part of the humiliation of punishment; a certain frisson might not always be out of place, if not improperly acted upon. In fact, the risk of impropriety itself provided an excuse for public rather than private rituals of corporal punishment.

The Old School Bench

What this means is that the Victorians and Edwardians were indeed sick puppies who applied non-consensual beatings. But, contrary to our image of them, they weren't always in denial about the eroticism of it. Famously, at Eton, its headmaster Keate was a particularly enthusiastic flogger. The standard and most painful of CP instruments was the birch, traditionally twelve birch branches bound at one end, and flogging blocks were placed throughout the school. A birching was carried out in public, the 'miscreant' given plenty of notice in which to contemplate the forthcoming event. Boys readily witnessed each other's humiliations, yet all were subject to them. Swinburne (see pp. 162–6), who was to say the least well aware of the sexual connotations of discipline, thought this was democratic, an equalising factor. To us it's basic, infuriating divide-and-rule.

At Eton, every pupil would have known the abject ignominy of a beating, from any age upwards of seven years old, and this was true of most public schoolboys up to World War II. The most poignant piece of writing on corporal punishment – as on many subjects – comes from George Orwell, who wrote in his 1947 essay *Such, Such Were the Joys* of being a young boy at Crossgates prep school, trapped in a bewildering cycle of bedwetting and beating:

'To this day I can feel myself almost swooning with shame as I stood, a very small, round-faced boy in short corduroy knickers, before the two women. I could not speak. I felt that I should die if "Mrs Form" were to beat me. But my dominant feeling was not fear or even resentment: it was simply shame because one more person, and that a woman, had been told of my disgusting offence.'

This essay was written late in Orwell's career. Perhaps it was only his awareness of the coming end of his life that made him call to mind this powerful shame at all.

Blazing Saddles

Back in the mid-nineteenth century, the fathers of Eton schoolboys could enjoy the constitutional invigorations of London's dominatrices as easily as they could have done in the 1990s. The most famous of these was Theresa Berkley, whose 'Berkley Horse' was a piece of equipment worthy of a modern bondage loft: an elaborate padded frame for flagellation, with an opening to allow fellatio on its bound occupant. This device was well reported in Victorian society pages, and some of these dominants were society figures themselves in the way that a porn star might possibly be today: rather naughty but acceptable as long as she remained a success story. Then, as now, these professionals were careful to distinguish themselves from the ordinary prostitutes of places such as Whitechapel – theirs was a hands-off, therapeutic service, not a grubby economic necessity. They offered a quality experience, for 'the quality'.

At the more affordable end of the market for CP, small ads appeared in popular gossip magazines such as *Society* offering similarly physically beneficial services, for both sexes, alongside other, rather quaint health products such as Albion Milk and Sulphur Soap. These are some that appeared in 1899:

Discipline Treatment for Ladies Only
Japanese Treatment – Madame Lilly
School of Modern Discipline by Augusta Montgomery
Electric Baths; Manicure and Discipline Treatment.

Incredibly, there was a myth that flagellation was a beneficial treatment for rheumatism, and masochists might refer to themselves as rheumatics when answering such ads. Some of the vendors made home visits.

Bound Books

There was a huge amount of flagellatory literature, some home-grown and some in translation from mainland Europe. France had an image of louche decadence, and so many of these supposedly autobiographical tales were – or purported to be – French. Walter's *My Secret Life* and *The Autobiography of a Flea* both feature lurid accounts of the beating of miscreant maids. Living in a stiff, taxonomic era, some Victorians, such as Pisanus Fraxi, author of the extensive *Index Librorum Prohibitorum*, were drawn to catalogue all this erotica. Material featuring flagellation could be passed off, with a nod and a wink, as inquiring or campaigning non-fiction to those in the know, such as the book featured in this ad:

'Flagellation in Germany: under the title of *Nell in Bridewell* the advertiser begs to notify that he will issue immediately the first English translation of W. Reinhard's *Lenchen im Zuchthaus*, famous for its exposure of the brutal corporal punishment system once dominant in the Female Prisons of Southern Germany. The work is printed on hand-made paper, has been Englished by University men, and persons who write now will be supplied at the price of 10s per copy.' (*Society*, March 1900)

Certainly the nineteenth century smacked of hypocrisy in contrast to the clued-up days of the eighteenth, with its masquerading and playful partying. In 1735 a Georgian wit could proclaim in *The Gentleman's Magazine,* 'I have seen a Professor foam with Extacy [sic] at the Sight of a Jolly Pair of Buttocks!' No such plain-speaking was to be had in Victorian correspondence. From the middle of the century, the broadsheet newspapers increasingly carried correspondence from those wishing to abolish CP, which drew attention to psychological harm and even sexual abuse for the first time. Institutional CP had its puffed-up defenders, too.

Readers' Letters

Meanwhile, however, scandal sheets such as *The Rambler's* and *Bon Ton Magazine* carried a century's worth of coded, pornographic flagellant correspondence that was clearly intended to arouse. It pretended to take part in the abolitionist debate, most correspondents proclaiming themselves either for or against before explaining their reasons with a lurid, explicit tale of educational or judicial punishment, such as the following, which appeared in 1873, from one 'Fanny Quintickler', which includes the common element in CP stories of humiliating exposure:

'. . . the smart of the new birch caused the young culprit (a remarkable fine boy) to plunge and twist his body in such a manner, as to show a curious little thing, to the no small diversion of the schoolgirls. The young schoolmistress, however, having observed a pretty big girl, very busy in making the others remark – *what do you call it* – took her to a closet just by the school, where she gave her an excellent whipping.'

This flagellant correspondence differs little in principle from the kind of ersatz problem pages one might find in a modern pornographic magazine, which present explicit fantasies – from being caught in auntie's *directoire* knickers to dogging in Lovers' Lane – as genuine readers' correspondence that requires an answer. Many of the misunderstandings about the Victorians, such as that table-leg myth, were made by historians who took this pornographic correspondence literally.

Upstairs ...
When it comes to boys, as we've seen, anyone who was anyone was birched, darling! Swinburne's flagellant tutor, the Reverend James Leigh Joynes, was pictured in *Vanity Fair* on his retirement, trademark birch in hand. Winston Churchill was motivated by vivid memories of school beatings to institute a Parliamentary Committee whose report, in 1913, increased awareness of the abusive aspects of corporal punishment. What about girls? Did they get it as badly as you would think from Victorian fiction? Victorian and Edwardian pornographers made every effort to convince their readers and themselves that girls were flogged just as soundly in British public schools as boys, although evidence suggests otherwise. In 1908, a report of the Schools Inquiry Commission found no evidence of birching *or* CP in girls' private schools.

... Downstairs
It was a different story, however, for the daughters of the less affluent. Girls in asylums (workhouses), charity schools, Reformatory Schools and Industrial Schools could expect to receive CP, usually with a folded belt on the hands and shoulders. As late as February

1900 the London School Board heard a report that a certain girls' Industrial School had only just passed a resolution that girls over thirteen should be birched only on their shoulders. Prior to this they had suffered the indignity of being birched on their bottoms. Institutional use of the birch was not officially banned in mainland Britain until 1948.

The broadest truth of the unerotic and terrifying reality of institutional CP in Britain was that, contrary to all the fetish clichés, the poor, as ever, got it hardest.

Six Of The Best CP Facts

- The traveller and scholar Henry Spencer Ashbee, known as Pisanus Fraxi (1834–1900), left his famous collection of Victorian flagellatory erotica to the British Library. His grandson visited the Library and wrote that it had 'kept some eight thousand volumes . . . and let us hope will destroy a certain number which can be of no service to anyone on this Earth.'

- It is impossible to be shamed when not observed. 'An ashamed person can hardly endure to meet the gaze of those present, so that he almost invariably casts down his eyes or looks askant [sic]' (Darwin, *The Expressions of Emotion in Man and Animals* [1876]).

- Krafft-Ebing (1840–1903) mistakenly associated submissive and dominant tendencies with female and male characteristics specifically: 'This renders it intelligible that the masochistic element is so frequently found in homosexual men' (*Psychopathia Sexualis*).

- As late as 1976, Patrick Cormack, a Conservative MP, said in a Commons debate, 'People who have the future of our children truly at heart will agree that there is something to be said for the old adage that if one spares the rod one spoils the child.'

- The Old Testament was frequently cited in defence of beating: 'Withhold not correction from the child, for if thou beatest him with the rod, he shall not die. Thou shalt beat him with the rod, and shall deliver his soul from Hell' (*Proverbs* XXIII: 13, 14).

- In *The Naked Ape* (1976), Desmond Morris develops a theory that the uses of corporal punishment as discipline and pleasure both derive from exposure of the vagina or anus, echoing a primeval offer of sex as a way of defusing aggression.

MEDICAL PUNISHMENT

Enemas for Breakfast

Today, Dr John Harvey Kellogg (1852–1943) is best known for the breakfast cereals that he invented. Their huge commercial success, however, has obscured the man. Whereas KFC are happy to use the grinning, down-home face of a notional Colonel Sanders to vouch for the Southern authenticity of their chicken, a brief look at the life and concerns of Dr Kellogg shows you why Kellogg's, instead, opted for Tony the Tiger.

Kellogg elevated the alimentary canal to a godhead from one end to the other. At his sanatorium on America's East Coast, he prodded and purged. On the one hand he extolled vegetarianism and roughage for healthy stools – Dr Atkins he wasn't – and on the other, he administered enemas, experimenting enthusiastically with different temperatures and volumes. His patients' regimes involved enemas daily and sometimes more often, administered through nozzled contraptions of valves and rubber tubing that he had invented for the purpose; the treatment doubtless removed digestively 'healthy' bacteria from the rectum. He was a health enthusiast and lifestyle radical who became, with turn-of-last-century American alacrity, the P.T. Barnum of medicine. His faddism was pastiched in Alan Parker's 1994 film *The Road to Wellville*.

Kellogg is nowadays regarded as a crank, a textbook case of the enema-loving paraphilia of klismaphilia, although he was in his time viewed as a campaigner for health and sexual 'temperance'. We might now see him as a man who diverted his entire sexuality into receiving enemas and inflicting them on others. The humour is in the denial, enemas being all well and good between the consenting if gullible. But there's a darker side to Kellogg: it's one thing to deny your own sexuality but another to proscribe it in others. Well known for his pseudoscientific views, he took a firm line on 'sexual incontinence' and 'self-abuse', especially in young boys.

No Fun Allowed
Kellogg was by no means alone. As nineteenth-century physicians knew, the movement of a foreskin makes it easy to masturbate without lubrication. Depending on its degree, this lubricating function can be absent after circumcision. Circumcision arose in a variety of cultures for a variety of reasons, and many indigenous peoples such as New Zealand's Maoris – who have influenced today's primitives and body-modifiers – practised pubertal circumcision as a rite of passage. Non-religious circumcision in English-speaking countries, however, arose in a climate of sexual fear, especially concerning masturbation. It was then rationalised after the operation was already widely practised, so that 55 per cent of American male babies today are still unnecessarily circumcised, down from near universality throughout the 1960s.

The original reason for the operation was to control 'masturbatory insanity' – the range of mental disorders that were believed to be caused by the 'polluting' practice. Treatments ranged from diet and moral exhortations to hydrotherapy, physical restraint, frights and punishment, as well as surgery. Some doctors, according to the social historian Roy Porter, recommended covering the penis with plaster of Paris, leather or rubber; others cauterisation, chastity belts, spiked cock-rings and, *in extremis*, castration. At the same time circumcisions were advocated on men, clitoridectomies (removal of the clitoris) were also performed for the same reason, and America's Orificial Surgery Society for the advocacy of female circumcision operated as late as 1925.

Naughty Nurses

On a happier note, it's easy to see how the naughty nurse became a fetish archetype. From Barbara Windsor popping out of her costume in the *Carry On* films to the stylised 1940s images of pharmaceutical advertising or the TV drama *No Angels*, nurses are always going to be a turn-on. Like much else about fetishism, nursing has its roots on, or at least near, the battlefield. As such, nurses ministered more or less exclusively to men. Ignoring the fact that much military nursing has historically been carried out by other men, the Florence Nightingale image taps into a deep vein of male Madonna-worship, from which comes the association of nurses with angels. Nurse's uniforms emerged not only for hygiene – the cap and the apron – but for easy recognition, which could make the difference between life and death for a profusely bleeding soldier brought hurriedly to a dressing station.

You Give Me Fever

So far so virtuous, but whether in civilian or military life, nurses have historically, traditionally, been single, an edge of availability which completes the Madonna/whore equation, however unsound that may be. After all, meeting someone in a situation where your endorphins are flowing and you're in need of help can easily lead to the impression of a bond being made, however one-sided that may be. And unlike sex, when receiving medical attention you're not required to reciprocate, another plus-point for the self-centred sensationalist in all of us. There is still a rash of ironic advertising images of nurses, complete with white uniforms over tight curves, a perky cap, and maybe even some rubber gloves, a syringe and a come-hither smile. **Here's a list of the top five iconic pervy nurses from the past 40 years:**

5. Ooh Matron!
Hattie Jacques' Matron in *Carry On Doctor* (1967) is camp and comedic – female authority with a fuller figure. Her tyrannical attempts to keep nurses Joan Sims and Barbara Windsor in line are repeatedly flawed by Frankie Howerd's dishonesty and Sid James's roguishness, in one of the classics of the series.

4. Medication Time
Based on Ken Kesey's stage play and novel, Milos Forman's 1975 film *One Flew Over the Cuckoo's Nest* features Louise Fletcher's controlling, vicious Nurse Ratched, a dominant medical authority figure who's all the more scary because she thinks she's acting in her patients' best interests.

3. Blink 182
Juvenile punk-pop band Blink 182 tickled the funny bone in 1999 with their album *Enema of the State*, which features a comely, pervy nurse on the cover – all cleavage and cute cap, suggestively snapping on a rubber glove.

2. Come Play with Me
British sex comedy goddess Mary Millington starred in this, the longest-running movie in British cinema history, which ran in London's West End for nearly four years from 1977 to 1981. A saucy comedy set in a health farm, it broke cinema box-office records. The drawing of Mary as a naughty nurse on the film poster became one of the defining images of 1970s cinema in the UK.

1. Time for Your Greasing, Mr Marlowe
When Michael Gambon has his genitals greased by a young Joanne Whalley in the BBC's original production of Dennis Potter's *The Singing Detective* – her half-knowing face framed prettily by her

nurse's collar and cap – he struggles to think of something – anything – that will stop his tumescence.

THE WEIMAR REPUBLIC (1920–1933)

After the convulsions caused in Germany's imperial government by her surrender in World War I, the country was governed by a parliament based in the town of Weimar. Berlin, meanwhile, became a thriving focus of artistic activity and social experiment. It rivalled Paris as Europe's cultural capital, and became a Mecca for artists and writers from around the continent.

The clean functionality of Bauhaus design was envisioned here, and the mordant political satire of Bertolt Brecht and Kurt Weill found its audience. Responses to the war came in the nightmarish expressionist drawings of Otto Dix and Max Beckmann, and from Erich Maria Remarque, writer of *All Quiet on the Western Front*. Life in 1920s Berlin was frightening: inflation reached three hundred per cent, and no one knew what cataclysm was coming next.

In this climate, Berliners kept dancing. Their clubs and *kellers* were fantasy spaces for exploring archetypal sexuality figures, transvestism and gender possibilities, from thigh-booted drag queens to well-tailored drag kings. Dietrich's top hat in von Sternberg's *The Blue Angel* (1930, see pp. 125–26) is an allusion to this. And let's not forget the cute appeal of blonde-pigtailed Bavarian *mädchen*.

The city between the wars was a fairground of fetishistic escapism and sub-dom role-play. Dominatrices led their slaves around for free – latterday Sacher-Masochs who could no longer afford the going rate. There were different establishments for different sexual orientations. Uses of leather and fur established fetish styles which are universal.

Amid this ennui and abandon, Christopher Isherwood, in Berlin with his lover Auden and working as a private tutor, wrote the novel *Mr Norris Changes Trains* and a series of short stories called

Goodbye to Berlin, which formed the basis for the musical *Cabaret*. Berlin in the 1920s was a city full of political ferment which eventually led the Nazi Party to power, while Berlin culture mocked the illusion that things would work out for the best. But the 1920s was a time when Germany, like the citizens of Berlin, could have gone either way.

PUNISHMENT AND POWER DYNAMICS

Under legal statute all are equal, but some, as we know, have always been more equal than others. The power dynamics of the real world, with individual possibilities bounded by hard economic realities, where you can't afford to bring in the lawyers, have inspired fetish archetypes. The unquestioning servant does the bidding of a superior not necessarily out of respect for them, of which they may or may not be personally deserving, but out of loyalty to a greater order of things in which they 'know their place'. In this (Marx would have said 'false') consciousness, the superior is also serving, in their way, the greater society, and both are united in service to a perceived wisdom larger than theirs.

It's a generally masochistic tendency to find comfort in this fetishistic feudalism. 'Yes, M'Lady,' says Parker to Lady Penelope in Gerry Anderson's *Thunderbirds*, but then they are engaged in a fight to keep the Earth safe from hostile aliens.

You're in the Army Now

The inception of all social discipline, anthropologically, was military. When it comes to the life-and-death, zero-sum game of battle, we all understand the need to instill an unflinching desire not to let the team down. The vestigial sense of protection of one's people, of comfort in order, can be a strong impulse towards sexual masochism, just as one's willing indisposition can confirm that one's own strength isn't needed, giving a relaxing sense of order over chaos.

It's no accident that uniforms – or signifiers of one form or another such as the zebra skins of Masai shields – were similarly conceived for recognition on the battlefield. Just as sexual fantasies allow us a safe way to confront our fears, so fetishism can be a coping mechanism for the real dynamics of power. It's no surprise that military styles have been a favourite of fetishists and SMers.

Gay male military fetishists – for whom battalions, from Roman legionaries to the French Foreign Legion, have provided stylistic inspiration, to say nothing of the disciplinarian atmosphere, historically, of British barrack rooms – are able to take each other prisoner with much of the same equipment as would be used in the real thing. Military scenarios also present a masochistic opportunity to test personal endurance, similar to sports-masochism. Meanwhile, army uniform remains a clubtastic fetish option: on the one hand, you could invest in one of House of Harlot's sheer rubber Russian army uniforms; on the other, a visit to an army surplus store, and some old DMs, is a lot cheaper than a visit to a dedicated fetish emporium.

Law Enforcement Through the Ages – Naming and Shaming

In mediaeval Europe, shaming was the name of the punitive game. Before organised law enforcement, it was up to the mob to bring a suspect before a magistrate, and it expected to be rewarded for its pains with a guilty verdict. As any number of lurid books of criminal history will chronicle, Britain had the stocks, brank and ducking stool. The pillory came later to urban areas and town squares and was even used in the eighteenth century for the punishment of supposedly seditious writings. It was not unheard of for these occupants – such as Daniel Defoe, who spent a morning in a pillory in the City of London – to benefit from a show of public support and get a sympathetic reception.

Public humiliation, however, was particularly refined in mediaeval German states, where punitive shaming was viewed as a more humane option than the infliction of pain for minor or domestic crimes. Civil life was closely regulated in thirteenth- and fourteenth-century Germany, and the law had an opinion on supposed infractions that only fundamentalists, of one form or another, would say are its business, such as cuckoldry and scolding. It's not surprising that the main 'beneficiaries' of this legal correction were women. Shaming masks were a German modification of the brank or scold's bridle. They may or may not have included a painful tongue-depressor, but they incorporated ridiculous appendages such as animal ears and bells. The severity of a sentence depended on how long a victim would be required to wear the mask in their daily life.

Held Fast in the Shaming Mask
If the shamed person was not tethered in public then, like an electronic ankle-tag, part of the sanction lay in encouraging the victim not to leave their home. The mask was not removed, either through social control and the threat of further sanction, or through the application of technology to hold the headgear fast while the victim's other limbs had normal freedom of movement. Before the invention of locksmithing and separate keys, battlefield technology was adapted to punishment devices throughout Europe. With the invention of body armour came rivets, holes and pins to keep it in place in the thick of war. Shaming masks were fastened beneath the chin in the same secure manner as knights' helmets, which the wearer didn't want to be pulled off quickly, an ironic adaptation of protective clothing that might have caused the victim to reflect that they were enjoying protection under the law.

Collared and Chained
Similarly, hapless offenders might find themselves collared and chained for a period to a pillar in a German town square. A variation on this was the Shrew's Fiddle, in which a victim's wrists

would be held in front of them as if they were playing a penny whistle. For added humiliation, these pincer-like devices were occasionally worked into stylised fiddle shapes. Pinioning the arms this way meant that the device didn't require locking, and left the wearer's body wholly unprotected from judicial poking and prodding. In a world of walled towns and city-states, public shame was often a precursor to exile.

Lock, Stock and Barrel

Mediaeval European incarceration devices are characterised by the problem of not being easily lockable. In equipment such as the Scavenger's Daughter, which held all four limbs in an arduous supplicatory posture, the object is often to hold the hands away from hinges and pins which could be easily pulled open. Or else limbs would simply be fastened in such a way that conventional buckles could not be easily reached. In this way the absence of locks actually led to greater physical restraint. Many of these devices crossed from being restraints to methods of torture, a step on the way to the rack or *peine fort et dur*.

Showing Restraint

Restraints and body braces were fastened using chains which pulled shut: elaborate, lateral-thinking chain puzzles to which only the gaolers knew the easy solution. More permanent options involved hammers and rivets – imagine the psychological panic of being hammered semi-permanently into restraint. An incidental though not unintended factor was often the debilitating weight and discomfort of the restraints themselves. Leg irons in particular were often heavy, while a fifteenth-century prison in Edinburgh must have been proud of its high, iron-spiked collar.

Mediaeval metals have mostly oxidised and our knowledge of these devices is based on written accounts. In recent centuries, there has been a private leisure industry of custom-made mediaeval-style restraints, to the extent that some aged examples in provincial museums probably betray the odd anachronistically modern bolt if you look hard enough, and were never worn in anguish. Probably the best-known modern purveyor of these devices is Jim Stewart's Fetters. (Fetters also produce straitjackets inspired by medical and prison history, as do Regulation, while American company Medical Toys offer a more intimate selection of Whitehead gags, specula, restraints, traction equipment, braces, tubing, and even bandage and plaster.)

Cops and Robbers

Equally, today's SM-ers favour the use of real, contemporary handcuffs and restraints as supplied to the law enforcement and medical industries, and there is a collectors' market in the durable, professional nineteenth- and twentieth-century offerings of companies such as Smith & Wesson, Cumming and Carberry, in which, bizarrely, cops and straight-laced collectors bid against pervs on eBay. Meanwhile, companies such as Humane Restraint, an industry-standard law-enforcement supply company, sell a range of 'prisoner transportation' equipment – stretchers, neck-braces, spit-guards – enough to completely immobilise. Though most of these companies are more used to supplying on account to law enforcement and America's vast private prison industry, they're not out of reach of the private buyer, and for every happy submissive who is strapped into a set of such restraints, that's one less African-American who hasn't paid their library fines.

Closer to Home

The British may not think they're as crassly mediaeval in their approach to modern-day judicial punishment as the Americans, with their perp walks, court television and culture of public shame, but it's worth remembering that we're not that different this side of the Atlantic:

SHORT, SHARP SHOCKS

Three swingeing examples of Cruel Britannia:

- Genesis P. Orridge, of electronica pioneers Throbbing Gristle and Psychic TV, owned Emma Peel's original Atomage-designed catsuit from *The Avengers* until it was taken in a police raid. Now resident in New York, he has reportedly never had it back.

- In 1992, sixteen gay male SMers from London were sentenced to prison terms of between three and six years for consensual acts by the appropriately named Judge James Rant. On referral to the Law Lords, two of the sentences were still upheld. The Law Lords' ruling contains just about every popular misconception about SM.

- Two weeks after that ruling, the Met raided fetish club Whiplash, assuming that prostitution must be taking place because, well, people don't really enjoy that sort of thing, do they? It should be added that these less enlightened elements of the force seem to have since retired.

FETISH ICON: T.E. LAWRENCE (1888–1935)

SM Biker, Young Turk
(fetishes: sub-dom, CP, military, racial)

Clouds Hill is a quiet country cottage, modest in its time, but not overlooked. The former home of T.E. Lawrence, it is situated near Bovington Camp in Dorset, where he was stationed in the early 1930s – not, as you might expect, in a sinecure that reflected his status as the World War I hero Lawrence of Arabia, but under the assumed identity of Private Shaw. In one of the upstairs rooms, there is a single bunk bed made from mahogany with large utility drawers underneath for kit and bedding, such as you might have to painstakingly arrange as part of a punitive pack drill. The room is decorated with aluminium foil to look like the interior of a metal-hulled ship, and contains a circular porthole window, through which you don't expect to see the unspoilt Dorset countryside.

The 'music' room contains a homely fire grate, a gramophone with a large horn and some shellac records. In front of a folding-leaf table and Lawrence's typewriter stands a stool, which was a gift from Thomas Hardy's widow. Did Lawrence grip this as he bent for a caning at the hands of a young subaltern from Bovington Camp? Although corporal punishment was abolished in the British army in the nineteenth century, the term 'music', as slang for a beating, persisted unofficially until after World War II with threats such as 'I'll make music on your arse' or 'I'll make you sing'. It would have been impossible for Lawrence to have named the room without being aware of its army use.

Downstairs, in the 'book' room, is a large, leather-covered double bed. While there's no specific evidence that Lawrence took part in CP scenes at Clouds Hill, why else should a house be so perfect for pack-drill, cold baths and standing to attention, ordered beyond even the fastidiousness of the typical military man?

Though not quite the dashing warrior of legend, Colonel T.E. Lawrence was the most remarkable intelligence officer of his time. By his mid-twenties he had helped the Arab Revolt succeed against the Turks, securing oil and a land passage to India for Britain, through clever manipulation of his relationship with King Faisal. He went on to compromise Arab hopes of statehood at Versailles in 1919, when they had served their purpose and Britain was keen not to give colonial advantage to the French – 'better that we win and break our word, than lose.' Lawrence never personally got over the betrayal he delivered, and among his many masochisms were otherwise useless attempts to atone, such as his refusal to profit from sales of *The Seven Pillars of Wisdom*. The depths of his self-disdain are those of a man who had not only betrayed, but betrayed what he loved.

Like Sir Richard Burton before him, Lawrence's intelligence success overseas was born of an Orientalist fascination that was at least as sexual as cultural. Born in 1888, one of five illegitimate sons of an Anglo-Irish baronet, Lawrence had been frequently beaten by his mother. From 1911 to 1914 he joined an archeological dig on the banks of the Euphrates river. Here, he fell in love with a fifteen-year-old Arab peasant boy, Salim Ahmed, whom he called Dahoum. He brought him on holiday to England. The couple were inseparable until Dahoum disappeared in 1916. He was rediscovered in 1918 when he was found dying of typhoid. Dahoum's death would have been fresh in Lawrence's mind during his betrayal of Arab nationhood.

After the publication of *The Seven Pillars*, Lawrence began his bizarre life of self-abnegation, on the run from fame, success and identity. He was as made as any young Englishman of the period could be; all doors were open to him. He turned down both the Victoria Cross and a knighthood. Although he became a Fellow of All Souls College, Oxford, he ensured his military career remained in the ranks by twice going to the extreme length of assuming a new identity, first as Aircraftman John Hume Ross in the recently formed RAF and then, when his identity was discovered and he was quietly discharged, as a private in the Tank Corps, when he changed his surname finally to Shaw by deed-poll.

While in the RAF, he befriended another recruit, John Bruce, and inveigled him into giving him regular and proper birching sessions, with the traditional, lacerating instrument that has many branches, tied at one end. According to a story that couldn't have been hard for Britain's most gifted if currently underachieving intelligence officer to come up with, 'John Ross' had been a naughty boy and stolen money from an uncle, who had consented not to go to law provided that his nephew sent evidence that he had been in receipt of regular birchings until the amount was all paid back. Lawrence even showed him letters from this fictitious uncle. Bruce, it seems, was not participating other than to fulfil a strange favour, and later spoke angrily of Lawrence's 'flagellation disorder'.

A pivotal event in Lawrence's life, as in David Lean's 1962 film *Lawrence of Arabia* (which is based firmly on *The Seven Pillars*, of which Lawrence himself said, 'no one should mistake this narrative of mine for history') is his beating, torture and rape at the hands of the Bey (local commander) of Deraa and his men in November 1917, when he was captured by the Turks while scouting alone for a location at which to sabotage the Medina railway. Lawrence's own account is vivid and homoerotic and panders to British stereotypes of the Turkish enemy: the leering Bey; the fraternal sympathies of the Turkish soldiers who by turns join in the beating and then more privately minister to Lawrence's bruises, expressing their fear of the commander and their relief that it was not their turn tonight.

Lawrence was by many accounts a shadow of himself after World War I, but he betrays an attraction to what repels him, and an instinct for mythmaking which Robert Bolt took up for his screenplay for Lean's wonderful but highly imagined film. Historians remain divided over the truth of the Deraa incident. In letters to Charlotte Shaw, wife of George Bernard Shaw, a kindly matriarch who helped Lawrence find self-acceptance in middle age, he reproaches himself for having given his consent; but the family of the Bey of Deraa insist their grandfather was a solid citizen and not given to gay SM and desert lust, whether consensual or otherwise. How much Lawrence's sexual fascinations were his own, and how much a response to the events of his life, can never be known.

Up to the time of his tragic death in a motorcycle accident, Lawrence was continuing to write. *The Mint*, published posthumously, is a masochist's appreciation of life in the ranks of the RAF. Meanwhile his brother, Professor A.W. Lawrence, maintained that T.E. resorted to flagellation at times of emotional turmoil, during which he sought to achieve subjection of the body 'by methods advocated by the saints whose lives he had read'. The emotional turmoil lay perhaps in living in an age when he would only have been able to bring up those intense feelings as long as they remained attributable to events at Deraa.

Lawrence shunned the laurels and the power that were his due on account of his masochistic sexual nature. He continued to feel a crippling guilt towards the Arab people. His sense that his achievements in the Middle East were fraudulent was perhaps itself a function of his self-abnegating and submissive nature. Today, we might expect of a man of Lawrence's standing a degree of need for executive relief and a demand for submissive play typical of sexually submissive high-achievers who can afford paid domination – a fantasy of powerlessness before returning to reality. But Lawrence did not distinguish between fantasy and reality – he lived his submission like a samurai. Just as Lawrence's homosexuality made the social rewards of success seem hollow, as if laid on for a different man, so his fetish for being on the receiving end of corporal punishment – for sexual submission – confirmed him in a deeper wish not to be part of the great and the good – for social submission too. After his remarkable achievements, what luxury did he take from life? He became his own 24/7 lifestyle slave and his master was the military.

Lean's film was ranked third most popular British film in a BFI survey in 1999. Peter O'Toole's *kafiyeh*, dagger and swirling clothes, digitally remastered, will continue to effect a transformation similar to transvestism – a becoming Other, though this time the Other is the Arab, not the female. It's as if with the clothes comes the grace required to wear them, away from the chafing twill of the army uniform in which the real Lawrence of Arabia had always found his own masochistic comfort.

2: POWER DRESSING – FETISH FASHION ON THE CATWALK

UNIFORMITY

Our common conservative interest in maintaining social order has been inextricably linked with the history of clothing. We are all, in a sense, in uniform all the time, since clothing cannot help but give out signals about who we are. They are the 'face value' at which we ask to be taken. I will dress smartly when I need to give an impression of credibility. I may debate with myself whether or not to wear a tie. Alternately, I may dress down if I am buying a used car or visiting a dangerous place, so as not to give an impression of prosperity. People may surprise us, revealing themselves to be other than they appear, but that is because we have made presumptions in the first place.

It is impossible to step outside this envelope as long as we are watched. In *Being and Nothingness*, Jean Paul Sartre gives the example of a waiter. As he works, he has long since forgotten consciously that he is being looked at, but nonetheless behaves in the manner that diners expect. We all have our public and private selves, and most of the time we find it easiest to confirm others' expectations of us. We ordinarily cease to be aware that we are being our public selves, just as we cease to be aware of wearing our clothes. That is, unless either of them causes us discomfort.

Biker Chic

Orthodox rebellion is easily understood. In *The Wild One*, when Mary Murphy famously asks Marlon Brando, 'What are you rebelling against, Johnny?' she already knows he's a rebel – that much is already a given, he's no different from the waiter. His is a peacock rebellion, an expression of the blithe, wilful hormones of youth; a mating ritual, and therefore quite conservative, for it's a pose, the kind of acting up that settles down. All these Johnnies are rebelling against is having to do what they're told. Just like the real-life unhinged, borderline-psychotic former GIs who took over the northern California town of Hollister in the late 1940s, inspiring the film, Brando's Johnny doesn't have a manifesto or a list of demands. He simply relishes chaos and Dionysian excess, rather than a measured consideration of other people. He's out for kicks, not crucifixion. So Mary Murphy's character is hot for Johnny – she knows he's a rebel and wants a piece of the action. The black leather signifier must have connoted all manner of imagined sensations to a '50s apple-pie girl like her. Truly maverick behaviour is necessarily open to greater misunderstanding. Brando lounges jauntily on his bike on many a bedroom wall, his famous leather cap and jacket as much a uniform as a cop's, inspiring a million gay fantasies.

As long as we are observed, we will be interpreted. Even naturism makes a sartorial statement, and we form a reasonable expectation of someone's character and opinions based on the context of their nakedness, whether it's their own bathroom, a beach or festival, or the wicket at Lord's cricket ground. Likewise, an attempt to convey that clothing isn't an individual's priority, that they don't subscribe to what the fashionistas tell them they should wear, or go for designer labels, is still a sartorial statement, however Maoist. It still invites a particular response.

Meat Puppets

In displaying fashions at all, we are deciding to take control of how we're perceived. We dress in certain ways to invite certain responses from the world around us: to get a job, to go out on the pull. We even dress up to dress down, when the same element of choice is involved. In all contexts, we're complicit in the process of ordering society, just by giving cues for how we'd like to be understood. These are the invisible strings that tie our bodies to social bondage and disciplinary codes.

So what's particular about fetish fashion? By this term I don't mean everyday clothing that gives you a private thrill, but something designed, with a fetishistic sensibility. Fetishism provides a way of changing the signals we give, but also letting the viewer know that we're doing it. By pretending, we get to grab hold of our puppet-strings, and pull them in return.

Fetish fashion requires context, and a plan for the unplanned. To wear fetish fashion is to play with order to invite chaos. This is a fancy way of saying we dress up to have fun, but it also hints at *why* it's fun. There is room for the unexpected, for bucks, beaus and oafettes; those in touch with their inner satyrs; for a safe experience of controlled chaos; and for the boys who, as half-approving matrons say, will be boys.

Friend or Foe?
From warfare to the frontlines of customer-service, uniforms codify the responses we can expect from a person. In war, they allow for fast, life-and-death decisions. On the high street, they signify, sometimes demeaningly, that we can expect certain forms of help or admonishment – 'Would you like fries with that?' 'You can't park that car there.' School uniforms have traditionally been thought to induce a spurious communal pride, the first way that we learn that we are 'us' and they are 'them' – 'Up school!' – a model for the larger patriotism of nation-states.

Whether it's the ubiquitous blue tunic of China's cultural revolution or the broad-shouldered costumes of Soviet art, the left has also applauded uniforms as social levellers and signs of equality, while totalitarian regimes and fast-food restaurants embrace their inherent suppression of the individual.

Going both Ways
Uniforms, as obvious statements of power dynamics, give us a language to play with in which the body itself does the talking. 'In

order to derive pleasure from the humiliation of and exaltation of the flesh, one must ascribe value to the flesh,' said Simone de Beauvoir when writing about Sade. If the heights of consensual, cruel tenderness can be dryly described, along with cherishing and hugging, as 'ascribing value', then so can the wearing of a uniform. Uniforms are also defensive, and give the wearer a sense of protection and power. They can empower and support, like armour, as much as they oppress.

TAKE A DEEP BREATH ... THE CORSET

The limitations of our clothes can remind us pleasurably that we are wearing them. We accept that we won't be able to run as well in a pair of bespoke shoes as we could in some off-the-peg trainers. The corset, like the shoe, was one of the first items of clothing to be treated as a fetish, and it remains one of the most important fetish fashions. Corsets were common throughout the eighteenth and nineteenth centuries. Glenn Close's tight-lacing scene in *Dangerous Liaisons*, involving two lady's maids, is a reasonably accurate portrait of the physical life of a French aristocrat. The corset demonstrated wealth and leisure.

Note the Difference

It's necessary to distinguish between ordinary fashionable corsetry, as practised by most nineteenth-century women, and the very different minority practice of fetishistic tight-lacing, which overlaps with sadomasochism and transvestism. There's a crucial point to be made in any look at the history of fashion: we cannot assume that similar clothes are worn for the same reasons. Although most Victorian women wore corsets, they were not usually tight-lacers with sixteen-inch waists, any more than most women today wear fetish shoes with six-inch heels. Then, as now, a handful of corset manufacturers catered to a core fetish market, producing unusually small corsets for women and men.

Lace Her Tight

Feminism argues that the female body has been the site of disciplinary regimes, such as dieting and feminine dress, that are designed to make women docile and feminine, but it may have been inaccurate in seeing the corset as playing a central role in the oppression and objectification of women. Susan Faludi writes in *Backlash* that 'the fashion industry has produced punitively restrictive clothing and the fashion press has demanded that women wear them. "If you want a girl to grow up gentle and womanly in her ways and feelings, lace her tight," advised one of the many male testimonials to the corset in the late Victorian press.'

This quotation, however, comes from one of the most suspect sources – the infamous 'corset correspondence' published in the *Englishwoman's Domestic Magazine*. Between 1867 and 1874, *EDM* printed hundreds of letters on corsetry, often with a pronounced sadomasochistic tone. Many historians have uncritically accepted the bizarre accounts of tight-lacing in *EDM* as evidence of widespread corset-based oppression during the Victorian era.

In fact, tight-lacing was almost universally anathematised in the nineteenth century. The *EDM* letters and their successors are highly unusual in defending the practice, and are usually presented out of context. They are erotic material – it's as if future historians based their assumptions on the readers' letters of today's porn mags, and concluded that the vast majority of us had sex in public car parks.

Elegantly Waisted

Some fans of tight-lacing who wrote to the *EDM*, like 'Alfred', sadistically imagined female suffering: 'There is something to me extraordinarily fascinating in the thought that a young girl has for many years been subjected to the strictest discipline of the corset.' It was also common for correspondents to imagine young men who were forced to tight-lace at the hands of matronly women. Others were inspired to tight-lace themselves. One man wrote to *Modern Society* in 1909, 'I was persuaded ... to get a pair of corsets by a "Tortured Victim" with a waist of seventeen inches.'

Wilhelm Stekel, a sexologist contemporary of Krafft-Ebing, described several such cases, like that of a 'respectable' married man who tight-laced, cross-dressed and wore women's high-heeled shoes that were so tight he limped. 'It actually appeared as if physical pain were an integral part of his bliss and he gloated in it as long as it were caused by some feminine article of apparel.' Pain and compression were frequently described in the *EDM* letters as 'fascinating', 'delicious', 'superb' and 'exquisite'. Many stories were written from the point of view of an adolescent charge who is forced to tight-lace until the feeling becomes pleasurable and craved, not unlike the fantasies of modern SM literature.

Club 18–30
Nineteenth-century fashion corsets were usually advertised as eighteen to thirty inches. Larger corsets of 31 to 36 inches were also widely available, and some advertisements mention sizes of 37 inches and above. Ads promising waists of fifteen inches upwards appeared in magazines which, if we look again, are full of the coded irony of fetishists' correspondence. These magazines, if taken literally, betray every aspect of Victorian patrician archness. Corsets were worn for different, more or less intimate, reasons much as today. Misunderstanding has come from a failure to distinguish between fetish and fashion corsetry.

Strictly Fashionable
Stephanie Jones, writing in *Skin Two* magazine in 1989, observed, 'One might imagine that in the world of SM role-play, the corset wearer is always the submissive, the slave. But this is not true; the symbolism of the corset is more complex.' She goes on to write: 'The dominatrix wears her corset as armour, its extreme and rigid

curvature the ultimate sexual taunt at the slave who may look but not touch ... The slave, on the other hand, is corseted as punishment.' The corseted dominatrix looks and feels 'impenetrable'. By contrast, the corset for the slave reminds him of discipline and bondage. 'It simultaneously gratifies his wish to look like a woman, while punishing him and thus assuaging his sense of guilt.' Said dominatrix Alexis DeVille, 'All I know is if I wear a corset in a scene, it gets better results with a slave than if I'm not wearing it.'

Straight-backed

Many specialist erotic magazines carry fantasy correspondence, presented as fact, not unlike that which appeared in the *EDM*, whose correspondence often dealt with a perverse 'hidden academy' – the tight-lacing boarding school – where young men would be overpowered by sturdy *mädchen*. In reality, European men were not corseted unless they were fetishists. Only the dandies of the 1820s sometimes wore boned, laced corsets to achieve a fashionable figure, and they were so caricatured that it's hard to tell what the truth was. Otherwise, stays were worn for practical support in the army, when hunting or for strenuous work, and must have been about as arousing as those neoprene trusses that federal law requires American site-workers to wear.

De Beauvoir Town

It is also important to emphasise the long tradition in pornography of first-person female accounts that were in fact penned by male authors, such as John Cleland's *Fanny Hill*. In 1899, 'A Woman of Fifty' wrote to *Society* to describe her experiences at a finishing school in the early 1860s, under the stern tutelage of one Mme de Beauvoir, during 'one of the periodic cycles of tight-lacing, as may be gathered from the correspondence which appeared in the *Englishwoman's Domestic Magazine* about this time.' She referred to many of the cult elements that played a role in fetish literature.

There was the ritualistic title of the sexy and sadistic Mistress, Mme de Beauvoir, a governess with a thirteen-inch waist; 'Birching ... was an openly recognized punishment'; nipple-rings, an anachronistic detail since they were a turn-of-last-century fad, were worn by 'three French girls, daughters of a marquise'.

Then As Now

Though all of these activities were probably indulged in by Victorian fetishists, it's important to understand that only in fantasy are they presented as the norm. Apart from anything else, presenting sexual subject matter as a matter of fact quite simply legalises it for publication. Therefore, many of our ideas about those de-oxygenated, swooning Victorians are probably based on *their* sexual fantasies.

Private Thrills

During the Edwardian era, corsets went the way of the crinoline, and began to disappear from women's fashion. Dress became neo-classical, and hourglass figures less lusted-after. In fact, the correspondence of flagellant magazines at this time bemoaned their disappearance in public. By 1910, younger women began replacing the boned corset with a rubber girdle and brassière, while older or stouter women switched to a long, straight corset.

Throughout most of the century, the corset remained the preserve of fetishists, associated with sex and sexual perversion. The tight-laced actress Polaire, whose tiny waist was featured in *Tatler* and *Photo Bits* in 1909, was profiled again in *London Life* in 1937. The mainstream 'waspie' girdle of the 1950s was incorporated into fetishwear. In post-war America, the corset became a central fetish object in the art of Eric Stanton and John Willie, a natural partner for thigh-boots or heels. With their shorter length and ease of movement, waspie corsets are easily associated with dominance. They are also often front-fastening, so that the intricate lacing at the back can be tied to an ideal width, and the corset easily put on and removed with a brief intake of breath. By the 1960s, early custom-fetish clothing manufacturers such as Atomage were combining corsets with catsuits. Corsets had by now become fit for rehabilitation by *haute couture*.

Twentieth-Century Foxes

What really distinguishes the corset as a fetish fashion garment is when it is worn on the outside, or at least visibly, if nothing else is being worn. In this way, it was reintroduced to fashion during the 1990s. Candace Bushnell, creator of *Sex and the City*, wrote about corsets in the *New York Times* in 1994. 'The debate on whether corsets embrace or imprison may stir again as newfangled corsets are appearing on the streets.' The culprits were these:

- In the 1950s, French couturier Jacques Fath created a pink satin evening dress with corset lacing up the back.

- Vivienne Westwood was one of the first designers to exploit the charisma of the corset, following her 'pirate look', in 1985. Westwood was inspired by eighteenth-century stays, rather than the more familiar Victorian hourglass corset – 'Fashion always requires something new yet draws from the past.'

- French fashion designer Thierry Mugler made the corset an integral part of his *femme fatale* designs, modelled by Diane Brill in the 1980s. Mugler showed aggressive corsets with spiked breasts; leather corsets with nipple-attachments; women's plastic bustiers inspired by ancient Roman body-armour; and evening-wear corsets.

- The French designer and sometime television presenter Jean-Paul Gaultier designed Madonna's striking pink, lace-up satin corset with conical breasts. His influential spring 1987 collection featured a number of corsets, bras and girdles. He has also designed jackets for men and women with corset-style lacing up the back. Gaultier's signature perfume is packaged in a bottle modelled on one of his corsets. Gaultier recalls finding a salmon-pink corset in his grandmother's closet – 'I thought, "My God, what is that?" '

- Italian design house Fendi produced a corset bathing-suit in the 1990s.

Modern Corset Facts

Other notable designers who use corsets have included Tunisian-born Azzadine Alaiia, whose beautiful corsets include leopard-skin patterns and red leather, and Betsey Johnson, Chantal Thomass, Christian Lacroix, Ungaro and Valentino. Lagerfeld made corsetry a centerpiece of his work for Chanel, although more for an hour-glass shape than fetish influence. 'You can't wear these clothes without a corset,' declared Lagerfeld.

In the more straight-waisted, pierced-naveled twenty-first century, corsets remain a fetish icon. As club-wear, they are unsurpassed as flattering garments, adding a confident stride to an evening out. They also help preserve the posture required to balance in heels, while plastic 'bones' ensure they are lightweight. Any number of corset options are available, from the basic rubber, clasp-fastening versions from fetish clothing companies such as Skin Two, to a custom-tailored old-school boned corset from Rigby and Peller.

Corsetry is proving a hardy perennial, blooming once more with the return of burlesque. Exotic dancer Gwendoline says that a love of corsetry itself got her into burlesque, while Atsuko Kudo's playful patterned-rubber designs are taking fashion corsets somewhere new. Nicole Kidman's corset-clad Satine in Baz Luhrmann's *Moulin Rouge* has further laced the public imagination with a shapely waist.

RUBBER DUCKS

Pity the poor rubber fetishists of post-war Britain: clad in waders, rubber macintoshes or any workwear that may have come to hand, they had to make do with at least faintly ridiculous found objects to indulge their desire to be encased, enclosed or otherwise deliciously wrapped in their chosen set of tactile, visual and olfactory associations. Thanks to apologetic, non-explicit magazines (the whole point being to see *less* of the flesh of the rubber-wearing model) such as *The Rubberist* or *Shiny*, their predilections gradually came to the attention of clothing companies such as Atomage, and the fetish-clothing industry was born. So in a way we owe the modern, grandiose designs of House of Harlot or Paradiso to those pioneers who snapped on the Marigolds and that old wartime gas mask behind closed suburban curtains.

Rubberists also had to put up with the opinion of psychoanalysis, informed by Freud, that their pleasure must be due to childhood problems with bedwetting, perhaps involving rubber sheets or pants, and therefore be an infantile, arrested habit, even though the body-enhancing properties of silks and satins had been commonly accepted as erotic since before the seventeenth century, when Robert Herrick wrote:

> *Whenas in silks my Julia goes*
> *Then, then, methinks how sweetly flows*
> *The liquifaction of her clothes*

Then, once fetish culture was established, rubberists were derided by art and fashion students and clubbers as a perishable old guard. Malcolm McLaren referred to the middle-aged fetishists who happened upon his and Vivienne Westwood's King's Road boutique, Sex, as 'the rubber-duck brigade'. From another quarter, rubber was considered sexually objectifying by its constriction, as seen in some of the opprobrium generated by Allen Jones' rubber-look sculptures (see p. 89).

Skin, Too

Rubber clothing was invented in the nineteenth century, and from the beginning its uses were suggestively encasing – clothes were marketed for any job in which one needed to be waterproofed. An ad in a London newspaper of 1870 offered 'a gentleman's nightshirt with attached nightcap in Macintosh cloth'. It apparently enabled 'a free and healthy perspiration'. Macintoshes and sou'westers quickly established themselves in romantic literature, not least as they became associated with the new and dashing hobby of motoring.

It was not until the 1960s, however, that Yves St Laurent and Mary Quant adopted rubber and PVC (polyvinyl chloride) as mass-market fashion items. Cheap, accessible and effectively waterproof if sweaty, cheeky designs exploded on to the high street in a variety of colourful and patterned plastics. St Laurent pioneered the use of transparent plastic, too. They were cheaply sexy materials that had a wet-look, reflective coating which literally mirrored the appeal of the finest patent leather.

Wet-look

1969/1970 saw the brief fashion explosion that was wet-look. Rippled, crinkly plastic was fashioned into raincoats, wasitcoats and accessories (the 'soul' cap as worn by the early Jackson 5 was a popular addition) and, for once, it was any colour except black. Red, yellow, purple and even green were the favoured hues. Now never to be found in charity shops, those pervy raincoats must all have cracked and perished. Of course, once a brushed nylon underlay was seen to poke through, the fun was lost.

New Rubber

Rubber reappeared in the 1980s, generally in any colour so long as it was red or black, with high-tech, often spiky designs, not just used in clothing but accessorised for bags and sofas too. This semi-industrial look was pioneered by designers in the early *Skin Two* catalogues such as Ectomorph, Wild Designs or Murray and Vern. Now these designers were making clothes for a self-identified UK fetish scene that had been partly inspired by New York's leather clubs. Given how many media commentators like Ted Polhemus were club-goers at this time, it wasn't long before the fetish scene inspired the mainstream.

Shine On

When George Michael modelled a leather jacket and Levi's 501s on his *Faith* album, the gay-biker/Brando leather look had finally become safe and mainstream. Thanks to designers like Thierry Mugler, rubber was briefly involved. The late-1980s popularity of the ubiquitous, stretchy, clingy, Lycra-impregnated 'little black dress' meant that a few of them were rubber, too. In 1989, *Vogue* carried a feature entitled 'Skin on Skin', which showed clothes by Gucci and Chanel of supple, shiny Napa leather very similar in form-hugging appeal to rubber.

However, rubber itself, it seems, will always retain a seedy, cheap, sluttish whiff of sex, and something of the hardcore. It can never be denied as a source of a private, intimate thrill. From the heavy rubber of Submission and The Clone Zone, constricting, enforcing and mummifying, to the flimsiest diaphanous rubber panties and the submissive, tacky PVC of cheap maid and nurse aprons, costumes and caps, rubber is difficult to maintain and wear. It isn't hard-wearing, it makes you sweat, requires talcum powder and polish and is ruined by a single cigarette-burn. These factors ensure that rubber will always mark its wearer unambiguously as a fetishist.

Furverts

Furs, velvets and silks are good examples of how a sexual predilection may be viewed as a sexual fetish or not, according to time and place. Freud believed that fur and velvet symbolise pubic hair, where the male child – the fetishist – expects to see a penis.

These materials were considered the subjects of fetishes even when they were more commonplace. Nowadays we tend to see them as sensuous anyway. Silk nighties, velveteen, fake and not-so-fake furs have become so conventionally sexualised that they fuel only the most 'vanilla' fantasy.

Sacher-Masoch (see pp. 159–62) was the original fur fan. In *Venus in Furs* he writes, 'At the sight of her lying on the red velvet cushions, her precious body peeping out between the folds of sable, I realized how powerfully sensuality and lust are aroused by flesh that is only partly revealed.' The flesh is hard, sculptured, the folds of fur soft and flowing. Sacher-Masoch's interest is voyeuristic. In actual fact, however, and certainly in our own time, fur fetishism seems rather rare. 'Plushies', for example, fabled fans of their sexually abused soft-toy collections, seem – a little scarily – to be attracted not to the materials as much as to the very insensateness of their partner. Fur does have an important symbolic, transformative value, however, conferring a part-animal, part-Amazon status on the wearer. That, together with a legion of matinee, Tarzan-style, jungle B-movies, ensures that fake-fur bra-and-pants sets will remain staples of the buxom, burlesque exotic dancer. Fur reminds us of pubic hair? No – it makes us feel like feral, craven cats and dogs!

Flying Leathernecks

Leather has long been used to make objects such as harnesses, saddles and whips, as well as shoes, belts, jackets, blacksmith's aprons, armour, gloves and handbags. Leather clothing existed even before the Neolithic period, but leather has been a fetish material only since the nineteenth century, and most early accounts subordinate it to shoe fetishism. Early fetishists stressed the smell and shine of leather, with patent leather being particularly valued, but in the last century the symbolic value of the leather became more important.

Leather enters recent history thanks to the World War I flying ace, while there are numerous references to the history of the black leather jacket, and many photographic images of the Gestapo and the SS, senior Nazis in long black leather overcoats. The mystique of the motorcycle is also strongly associated with leather and sex. On a purely functional level, motorcyclists wear leather because of its durable and protective qualities. However, black leather has also long been associated with sadomasochistic sex for its own sake. In the 1920s and 1930s, pornographic photographs showed people dressed in black leather and engaged in SM activities. Not all sado-masochists are into leather, nor all leather-fetishists into SM, but there is considerable overlap.

Since the 1960s, the motorcycle culture that inspired *The Wild One* (see pp. 48–49) also inspired gay biker lifestyles. Although many leather fetishists are heterosexual, a significant gay 'leatherman' subculture also exists. 'Leather was gay sexuality stripped of being nice,' said the novelist John Preston. Larry Townsend's *The Leatherman's Handbook* contains a wealth of lifestyle advice for the gay leather-lover, based firmly on fraternal biker culture. Many of its earliest New York exponents believed in 'old-guard' values: part-ners didn't switch, and submissive and dominant lifestyles were biker-culture reality. The styles of this scene were adopted by performers such as Freddie Mercury or Judas Priest's Rob Halford, so that many stadium-rock fans in the 1970s were headbanging along to gay fashions without knowing it. In the 1970s and 1980s, a biker culture developed that was less literal, involving switching, piercing and a more modern-primitive, spiritual sexuality. This also interfaced with the as yet unrecognised gay skinhead scene, so that some sexual encounters pastiched the mod-and-rocker seaside violence of the 1960s. (Most appropriate, of course, in Brighton.)

Stormy Leather

Expensive *couture* adaptations of biker leathers in the 1980s finally made the material truly acceptable. Meanwhile lesbians too took to leather and, with some controversy, lesbian SMers and leatherdykes began to emerge from behind the veil of political correctness. Only within this community did it, for a while, retain its outsider status.

After we became familiar with Honor Blackman and Diana Rigg in leather in the TV series *The Avengers* (see p. 72), Yves St Laurent brought leather on to the catwalk. In the 1970s, Karl Lagerfeld's costumes for *Maîtresse* (see pp. 131–3) brought it into the public eye. In the later half of the decade, punk styles popularised the biker's leather jacket still further, until it was appropriated by Gianni Versace, Giorgio Armani and Donna Karan in the 1980s, and partnered naturally with denim, which was then resurgent in a number of new and different finishes. The leather jacket of Tom of Finland's drawings and greasy motorcycle toughs became a lilac suede blouson jacket.

Before rubber, leather was essential to fetishists interested in body-hugging possibilities. Naturally, these were only available to the wealthiest. Leather can be unsupple when cold, and does not fit as snugly as some twentieth-century artificial materials, which these days often replace it on the fetish scene. When worn, leather is valued more for its symbolic properties, perhaps as part of a uniform of some kind, than for its innate, creaking hints of pain, dominance and feral masculinity. As always, quality is everything, from cheaply tanned, grainy South American or Indian leathers to the most supple Italian Napa or patent finish. The real function of leather remains what it has been since primeval times, as footwear, and it will always be the material of choice for bespoke shoe design.

STEPPING OUT: FETISH FOOTWEAR

If style commentator and former Millennium Dome director Stephen Bayley believes that fetish fashion is naff, as he has said, then even he must surely make an honourable exception for shoes. While the clompy boots of tribal punk styles and cyberpunk may be a lazy option on the fetish scene, and the only other options for most of the 1980s were patent four- and six-inch stilettos and thigh-boots of a fairly homogeneous style, bespoke footwear remains an elegant, quietly spoken fetish. For chaps who enjoy good footwear, shoes can be like corsets for the feet, which really, after all, need corsetting and cossetting more than the average body part.

Today, fetish and bespoke footwear intersect, thanks to manufacturers such as Jeffrey West, whose quality products nonetheless retain a fetish edge, and shoeshops such as north London's The Little Shoe Box. Like sportsdykes, Lycra-lovers and military enthusiasts, shoe-fetishists enjoy the trappings of the everyday and not explicitly sexual. As high heels and kitten heels have made a return thanks to Manolo Blahnik and Prada, it's as if heels were never controversially identified with female oppression.

Hell on Heels

Social commentator Ann Magnuson described the agony and ecstasy involved in the cult of high-heeled shoes: 'What makes us different from the poor Chinese girls who were robbed of their mobility is that when we've had enough, we can walk away.' The four- and six-inch stiletto has been a paradoxical symbol of domination since the nineteenth century, and throughout the black-and-white porn of the 1940s and 1950s which informed the 1980s fetish scene. As in the debate about corsets, there is a comfort-versus-image issue: the extra height of heels confers imperious dominance at the same time as the shoe constrains the foot. This has been realised since cobblers first made raised heels for both sexes in the seventeenth century, partly to avoid the mud of urban streets.

Meanwhile, to the boot- and shoe-licking foot fetishist, it is not simply heels that remain objects of desire. Even unerotic strapped sandals have their fans, and one reason postulated by psychologists is worth attention: the toes, when constricted in a sloping, open-uppered shoe, form yet another symmetrical and mirroring cleavage, similar to the breasts, buttocks and even knees. In 1992, Chanel marketed cork-soled platform sandals with ankle straps, inspiring an article in the *New York Times* in which fashion historian Anne Hollander asked what was so 'sexy, perverse, and delicious' about this look. Musing about 'untold erotic practices', she suggested that an elegant ankle harness presents the foot as 'a beautiful slave'. Indeed.

VIVIENNE WESTWOOD OBE

A number of excellent fetish designers work in rubber to create fantastical clothes, House of Harlot and Paradiso to name but two. Fetish design has come a long way from the strict punk- and *Cabaret*-inspired image of A-line dresses, mini-skirts and tops that recreate high-street fashions in fetish materials, in any colour so long as it's black or red. Modern fetish design incorporates greater elements of roleplay than hitherto – you could be a pin-striped city gent or a 1960s airline trolley-dolly in sweaty rubber. Meanwhile, companies such as Regulation continue to tool supple, restrictive leather into adventurous styles.

Fetish materials are one thing, but if fetish sensibility is taken as the measure, then Vivienne Westwood OBE is the pre-eminent fetish designer. In the twenty-first century, it looks as if her styles, rather than the opening cadence of 'Pretty Vacant', could be the more lasting legacy of London punks. In spring 2004 a major retrospective of her work began at London's Victoria and Albert Museum. Westwood has been as inspired by eighteenth-century art –

creating a ball gown in homage to a Watteau painting – as by 1950s porn, which prompted her famous T-shirts of the late 1970s, featuring Tom-of-Finland-style illustrations and withdrawn from sale for obscenity.

'If you want to be original, you have to consider the past,' says Westwood. Although she came to prominence during the 'year zero' mentality of punk, her work is informed by an understanding that nothing is truly original, that someone has gone before. Coming soon after punk, her pirate look signalled this instinct early, modelled first by punk starlet Jordan (the original and best) but borrowed with greatest success by Adam Ant. In the mid-1980s it was Westwood's use of elastic and plastic stays that reintroduced the corset as an accessible and form-friendly fashion item. Any suggestion of objectification was irrelevant next to the obvious fact that Westwood's clothes existed for the pleasure of the wearer, and that sexual roles are empowering too. Westwood sums up her appeal as based on 'not the idea of sex but the idea of the heroine', and says that 'women need power as much as they need love'. She can't help it if heroics and power are sexy.

Couture designers such as Galliano and Lacroix acknowledge her influence, but Westwood's appeal is perhaps best hinted at by a recent design of hers – a body-suit with an eighteenth-century harlequin pattern. Westwood's chief influence remains the transformative times of the masked ball, and she does, indeed, make clothes that you could masquerade in.

FETISH ICON: BETTY PAIGE (b. 1923)

Danger Girl
(fetishes: fur, feathers, teasing, spanking, CP, bondage, suspension)

Today, hipsters listen to CDs of burlesque reviews, mix cocktails and enthuse over diaphanous gowns and feather boas, fake leopard-print furs and polka dots. American college girls sport

Betty Paige bangs. Her curves adorn badges, bags, T-shirts, CD artwork and even novels (Matthew Branton's *The House of Whacks*). Without anyone really noticing, throughout the 1980s and 1990s, first in fanzines such as *The Betty Pages* and *The Rocketeer*, Betty Paige became established as *the* fetish muse, the subject of fan-sites and art books. For most of the 1990s, the annual Glamourcon convention, dedicated to Betty and held in various US cities, drew thousands.

It would be amusing to say that Betty Paige, née Mae, arrived in New York in 1948 straight from the farm in a check shirt, chewing straw, talking in the sultry tones of a demure Southern Belle, wide-eyed at the city folks' ways. In fact, she came from the urban centre of downtown Nashville, left school as one of the smartest in her class and had a brief career as an English teacher and an equally brief marriage under her belt before heading for New York's Broadway with ambitions as an actor.

Short of money and game for a laugh, she began modelling for private camera clubs and, through them, for Robert Harrison, the commercial king of soft porn, or 'semi-nude', in 1950s America. Stacked in the rec room of a new tract home, magazines such as *Eyeful*, with its patriotic subtitle 'Glorifying the American Girl', were part of many hard-working American ex-servicemen's R&R, and still owed much to the fuselage art of the US Air Force.

Storyboarded spreads feature a scantily clad Betty playing dumb, pulling telegraphed silent-movie faces as she drives, flies or cycles, ending up in an ignominious heap of humiliation: 'Oh no, she's coming in for a crash landing! Next time maybe Gertie'll keep her mind on the steering wheel! It's a long road back home, and a dizzy dame like Gertie is skatin' it, fellers!' Harrison obviously knew better than to overestimate or threaten his less able readers.

More famously, though, Betty posed for Irving and Paula Klaw, former booksellers who had got into smut. They began to distribute burlesque films and photosets of 'artistic figure studies' by mail order. Betty featured in three full-length films of burlesque revues made by the Klaws, including the fabulous *Teaserama* with Tempest Storm (1955) – 'New and Naughty!' But anything that eased the pressure for darker pleasures in 1950s America had better be hush hush and strictly on the QT. The Klaws were soon being asked for material featuring bondage, spanking and whipping. Finding none, they began to shoot their own.

Betty's work with them was typified by the grainy black-and-white photo sets which feature inventive bondage in hammocks, across stools, hogtied in a hotel or suspended from a beam in a studio. Betty is by turns gagged with ball gags or cloth. Some feature bound cat-fighting conducted with obvious hilarity, while others are darker, featuring heavy cuffs, collars and chains, and mediaeval stylings, which in 1950s America meant something that looked like the interior of a steakhouse. Most feature seamed stockings and mostly black, occasionally frilly 1950s lingerie of the kind that is truly engineered, which frames bodies so well it becomes another layer of bondage, gauzy and strapped. Though it just reflected its time, it's a style of lingerie that has come to timelessly denote fetish.

Paige worked with Bunny Yaeger, herself a former model, and their topless shoots show Betty radiant in the Florida sun. They couldn't be more different in style from the Klaw pictures – being outdoor and colour rather than indoor and grainy black-and-white – and yet each has a similar level of rapport, on occasion the same open-faced smile from Ms Paige, and always the same sense of direct communication with and approval of the viewer.

Whether grinning or scowling, Betty is always mugging, playfully exaggerating herself. In photo sets where she binds, beats or otherwise tops another model, she is a sleeves-up, no-messing-about dom. As a sub, she is a matinee victim, batting her eyelashes, furrowing her brow. Whichever, it seems she was never far from a fit of the giggles.

By turns a wholesome Nashville hayseed or a siren from a twilight Times Square world, Betty Paige abandoned modelling in 1957 for a life of privacy, partly thanks to the Klaws' prosecution by the FBI for their mail-order activities. But in her decade of work, she established herself as the fetish übermuse.

There's a happy postscript to Betty Paige's story: in 1998, an intrepid documentary-maker tracked her down to a Los Angeles retirement home. Legal moves were then instituted to channel some of the revenue her image has produced in her direction. More importantly, however, she learned that she had become a sex symbol, and the thinking bi-girl's Marilyn Monroe, about which she had had no idea: 'It just surprises me . . . They keep saying I'm some kind of icon and that I started the new generation's sex movement. All I did was pose in the nude.'

3: PLUG ME IN: FETISH IN ADVERTISING AND ON TELEVISION

COMMERCIALS

In the last decade, there have been a host of ads, either beamed into our homes or printed in magazines, and even a stiletto poised above a man's naked bottom on a billboard, which suggest that most of the UK's advertising industry spends its weekends kneeling for six of the best. Here are the top five finalists in the services-to-fetish award:

5. Altoids – Whole-page magazine ads for these devilishly strong and pleasantly retro mints have featured a 1950s siren with a smile. In some she wears a fur bikini, in others she is dressed like a little demon, brandishing a whip.

4. Boddingtons – A 1996 commercial for this popular northern bitter featured wig-wearing easy-listening popster Mike Flowers performing the 1960s hit 'Release Me' in a pervy nightclub where regulars are dressed in rubber and leather. As he sings on stage, a man at the bar has his pint snatched away by a whip-wielding clubber dressed as Catwoman, who then downs the pint. 'By 'eck, she's whipped me cream!' exclaims the jilted drinker. Concurrent magazine ads featured an alluring pint of Boddingtons with a whip curled around it: they were having a whip around, then.

3. Purdey's – Agency Barrett Cernis devised a campaign for Britvic, makers of Purdey's Elixir, a re-energising multivitamin drink which included a kicked-off pair of six-inch stilettos and the straplines 'Punishing Day' and 'Redemption'. These ads appeared mostly in the *Guardian* Weekend Guide, perhaps where you'd expect a few PC pervs to be looking for their entertainment. The ads also featured an internet address where you could, apparently, post stories.

2. Pot Noodle – In 2003, Britain's Advertising Standards Authority insisted that television networks remove a Pot Noodle snack commercial. The ad promoted a spicy curry flavour by drawing a parallel between the salutary burning effects of corporal punishment and hot foods. It featured a couple – a dress-shirted, moustachioed cad who realises with anticipation that he is about to get Pot Noodle punishment from a crop-caressing siren.

Some commentators observed that the ASA had been prejudiced: other ads in the campaign had been just as suggestive, with no problem. 'The Slag of all Snacks' featured a young punter being turned away by a series of – we assume – prostitutes because his suggestion of eating Pot Noodles together is just too filthy for them. This suggested that the curry-flavour ad had been singled out by the ASA purely for its perversity. People who regard SM as a sexual orientation in itself were offended. Meanwhile, Pot Noodle evidently believe correctly that no advertising will put their lad market off their snack: they have marketed a Mexican flavour with a character named Seedy Sanchez – rather close to its obvious inspiration, the ill-advised sexual technique known as the Dirty Sanchez.

1. Agent Provocateur – In autumn 2001, British television networks banned a saucy, fetishistic commercial for classy lingerie manufacturers Agent Provocateur. Darkly lit and gothic, like a scene in a subterranean club, the ad features pint-sized pop siren Kylie Minogue. Wearing a see-through bra, matching briefs and the company's sheerest suspenders, Kylie rides a red mechanical rodeo bull as gamely as a cowgirl, laughing in the face of macho danger. It's raunchy – the bull is fast, furious and takes no prisoners. If you thought Kylie was best appreciated by gay men, this will prove you wrong. *Men*, it says, *this bull could be you*. 'Banned' is too strong a word, of course – the inevitable decision was used as free publicity for an ad that was made for cinemas in the first place. It's still out there on the internet and probably still crashes servers throughout the City of London.

TV

From women-in-prison dramas (*Prisoner: Cell Block H, Bad Girls*) to hospital soaps (*Angels, No Angels*), there are all kinds of mainstream TV series that use fetish archetypes on television, but here are a few of the television programmes that are fetishistic in a different or more self-conscious way.

The Avengers

The Avengers is a stylish blend of espionage, sexual fantasy and quasi-science fiction, but all so terribly British. The original series ran from January 1961 to September 1969 – witty, sentimental, off-beat television with formula plots which, like Emma Peel's catsuit, are so dated they're timeless. Leaving aside *The New Avengers* and the 1998 film which became known as 'Weintraub's folly' (after its producer Jerry Weintraub), it's this series that has the fetishistic spin.

Much of the show's popularity was due to the pairing of Patrick McNee and Dame Diana Rigg as agents John Steed and Emma Peel. Tongue is always firmly in cheek – goofy mad scientists and fiendish enemy spies abound, requiring, at the very least, dapper smoothness from Steed and his Whitehall chums (British civil servants have always had a whiff of the pervy about them) and some leather-clad high kicks from Ms Peel. Catch Steed's fantasy sequence in the episode 'The Hellfire Club', in which Emma appears in corset and spiked collar, python curled around her torso, cracking a whip at a kneeling Peter Wyngarde. Passing swiftly over the 1970s reincarnation *The New Avengers*, which was less 'shaken, not stirred' and more 'about this many beans in every cup', it's small wonder *The Avengers* became one of the most popular television series of all time, eventually reaching audiences in 120 countries. The show also spurred a spin-off novelty single in 1966 entitled 'Kinky Boots', which became a Top 5 hit and is the name given to selected DVD compilations of the series.

Carry On

Much has been written about Pinewood Studios' *Carry On* films, which began in 1958 with *Carry On Sergeant* and will invariably be encountered on late-night television these days. A shining example of post-war British culture pushing its own boundaries, the famous saucy series of films grew out of *ITMA*, a wartime radio comedy show, but broadened to encompass *palare* jokes and seaside-postcard sauce. There are so many catchphrases that come from *Carry On* films that we've forgotten their origins.

A frequent source of laughs is the comedic cross-dressing, a staple of British humour going back to Elizabethan theatre. Peter Butterworth cross-dresses grotesquely in *Carry On Screaming* (1966), but it is the gormless, ungainly and lovable Bernard Bresslaw who is usually required to, reluctantly, as scheming Sid James' stooge. There is a scene in *Carry On Doctor* (1967) in which Bresslaw's character sees himself as a woman for the first time and is transfixed by how ravishing his reflection appears, at least to his own eyes. It captures a fleeting thrill that can only happen once.

Eventually eclipsed by the sexploitation offerings of the 1970s (of which the dire proof is *Carry On Emmanuelle* [1978]), overtaken by political correctness in the 1980s and simply, for a time, not funny, the *Carry On* phenomenon now looks like a slapstick fight at a fancy-dress party, a post-war variation on an age-old theatrical tradition.

Doctor Who

A BBC SF television series that ran between 1963 and 1989, *Doctor Who* influenced four generations of British children at teatime every Saturday. It remains a significant part of British popular culture, widely recognised for its creative storytelling. The show became a cult television favourite. Even its theme tune is historic, a benchmark piece of electronica by the boffins of the BBC Radiophonic Workshop, and the first commercial use of voltage-controlled pitch – the basis of music synthesis.

The Doctor is a Time Lord, a race from the planet Gallifrey, and is not subject to the normal constraints of mortal life. His first incarnation was played by the grouchy William Hartnell, later to be followed by seven more, perhaps the most enduring incarnation being the fourth Doctor, played by Tom Baker. You can date a middle-aged British man, gay or straight, by which of the Doctor's assistants he had his first crush on.

The Doctor famously travels in his vehicle called the TARDIS (Time And Relative Dimension In Space), which enables him to travel to any point in time, anywhere in the universe. For the most part, he explores the universe at random (usually because the vessel's navigation system is old and unreliable), using his extensive knowledge of science and advanced technology to heroically avert crises on various worlds. The weekly episodes would form part of a contained story or serial of up to eight episodes. More epic stories that were essential to the Doctor Who myth, such as 'The Trial of a Time Lord', would last longer. The Doctor is accompanied by up to three companions: people who choose to travel with him for a period, for a variety of reasons.

Doctor Who was initially devised by the public-service, Reithian BBC to be educational. Some episodes would see the characters travel to important periods in human history. However, these historical stories were soon dropped in favour of SF flights of fancy. A wise move. *Doctor Who* is fetishistic on account of the strange and beguiling relationships the Doctor – always a rebel and a man of mystery – has with his assistants, and also because of the strangely suited but always powerful and sinister monsters.

Most of the show's mythology and backplot was developed gradually by later writers. At first, nothing is known of the Doctor at all, not even his name: in early episodes he is referred to as 'Grandfather' by the character of Susan. Barbara Wright, a teacher who later becomes one of the Doctor's companions, refers to 'The

Doctor' and Ian Chesterton, her fellow teacher at Coal Hill School, addresses him as 'Doctor Foreman', because the junkyard in which they have found him has the name 'Foreman' outside. The Time Lord responds 'Doctor who?' Hence the series' title.

In many of the stories, The Doctor has also saved the Earth (and a number of other worlds) from such notable adversaries as the Autons, the Cybermen, the Sontarans and the Silurians. However, the factor that probably did most to capture the public's attention was the introduction in the second storyline of the Daleks: a lethal race of metal-armoured mutants, whose chief role in the great scheme of things would appear to be, as they frequently observe in their instantly recognisable metallic voices, to 'Exterminate!' Later Dalek storylines introduced their fiendish, twisted creator, Davros, part Golem and part Ernst Blofeld.

Incredible though it may seem, for its time the show was actually scary, and there was some controversy over its suitability for children. Moral campaigner Mary Whitehouse made a series of complaints to the BBC over its sometimes gory content. Her actions couldn't have been better PR, giving the programme a certain cachet that made it even more popular, particularly with children. In addition to the seven doctors of the original series, there was a one-off 1996 television movie in which The Doctor was played by Paul McGann (and in which British luminaries such as Jim Broadbent, Joanna Lumley and Richard E. Grant appeared). Meanwhile, the *Doctor Who* franchise has spawned a host of graphic novels and comics, together with a long-running series of original fiction using the Doctor as a character, beginning with the Doctor's seventh incarnation but going on to tell 'untold' stories from the earlier ones.

Another feature that made the series so enduring was written into the Doctor's 'mythos' as it went along: he is a shapeshifter. Time Lords can survive injuries that would kill a human but, in doing so, they may change their outward appearance, and their natures too. They can do this only twelve times, however. One of the Doctor's adversaries, The Master, is a Time Lord who has gone bad – he's on his twelfth roll of the dice and will do anything to survive. As BBC Director of Programmes, Michael Grade finally killed off the Doctor before his turn was up. At the time, perhaps he had a point: *Doctor Who* was becoming a little risible, although thankfully *K9 and Company*, a spin-off series featuring the Doctor's robotic dog, never made it beyond the pilot stage.

Many aspects of the Doctor continue to appeal, not least that he avoided violence where he could, using cunning and ingenuity against brutish (and sometimes, it has to be said, conveniently slow) foes. Always deceptively scatty, with a down-at-heel manner masking his acute intelligence, and working with sub-standard equipment, his character is really a celebration of the classic British boffin who has spent a lifetime in his shed, twiddling with radio receivers.

One famous *Who* writer was Douglas Adams, author of *The Hitch-Hiker's Guide to the Galaxy*. In September 2003 it was announced that the Doctor will materialise again on BBC 1, in a series written by *Queer as Folk* creator Russell T. Davies, whose first published work was a novel in the *Doctor Who: New Adventures* fiction series. Mark Gatiss of *The League of Gentlemen* (see p. 97) is another writer on the series, while the Doctor himself will be played by Christopher Eccleston, who appeared in *Shallow Grave*. Will Baker, stage designer of Kylie Minogue's 2002 'Fever' tour, turned to *Doctor Who* for inspiration: 'I loved the movements of the Raston warrior robot – they were so balletic.' There is clearly a sinister, conspiratorial network of Whovians out to ensure that our Time Lord friend visits planet Earth – or, more specifically perhaps, a disused quarry in Hertfordshire – in the twenty-first century.

The Perils of Penelope Pitstop

Produced by Hanna-Barbera as a spin-off from the popular kids' cartoon *The Wacky Races*, *The Perils of Penelope Pitstop* featured breathy Southern Belle Penelope and her adversary, the seemingly kind Sylvester Sneakly, who is in fact ... the Hooded Claw! Making her debut in 1968, our plucky heroine escapes the ropes and traps of villain Sneakly, who wants to get his hands on her vast fortune. Each time, The Ant Hill Mob, Penelope's own Seven Dwarfs, try to rescue her from the sticky end Sneakly has planned, but pink-clad Penelope usually ends up rescuing herself. Inspired by silent films, she is trapped in the jungle or tied to railway tracks in episodes like 'Jungle Jeopardy' or 'Boardwalk Booby Trap'. Sneakly never did get her money but, voiced by the camp, sinister Paul Lynde, he ever-so-slightly tilted a generation of children towards moral turpitude while he tried. A silly, subversive offering that's just a little more unhinged than *Scooby Doo*.

Blake's 7

Blake's 7 was a major science-fiction television series made by the BBC between 1977 and 1981. Terry Nation, its creator, was also centrally involved in *Doctor Who*. The series ran over four seasons with a total of 52 episodes. It featured the exploits of a group of interstellar fugitives and their efforts to inflict serious damage on a vicious, corrupt and totalitarian galactic federation. It was a massive hit, with more than eight million viewers regularly glued to the adventures of this rebellious crew as they cruised the galaxy in their stolen, state-of-the-art craft *The Liberator*, on the lam from the federation.

The plots featured bitchy intrigue worthy of the Borgias, while the series so appealed to children that *Blue Peter* taught them how to make a teleport bracelet with sticky-backed plastic. Meanwhile, the cast drew out every cruel syllable of the camp melodramatic scripts, bringing a pervy fascination to their political cruelties with a relish that looks at *Star Wars* from a great height. With the imperious 'Supreme Commander' Servalan at the helm, the scene was set for a variety of wildly entertaining sub/dom relationships on board the Liberator. With her signature close-cropped black cap of hair and space-tastic off-the-shoulder gowns, she cut a fabulously haughty figure. There was also the plebeianly named but well-spoken rebel Del Tarrant, and the suggestively monickered Dayna Mellonby, often seen sporting spiked collar and silver space suit. *Blake's 7* featured lines like: 'Summary execution is the usual penalty for boarding a Federation ship without authority' or 'I am President and Supreme Commander of the Terran Federation. I want to see a senior official and I want to see him here now.' Such melodramatic posturing wouldn't be out of place in a fetish club.

The maximum pervy points, however, have to go to Paul Darrow, who played Avon, the leading computer and electronic expert of the Federation. In tight-fitting black polo-neck and a studded leather jerkin jacket that predated Earth, Wind and Fire concerts, this stern and commanding dom-fantasy character was many a young girls' heartthrob at the time.

Blake's 7 was littered with pervy features all round, not least the obvious 'Slave', the master computer on the back-up ship *Scorpio*. Complete with fawning personality and low self-esteem, Slave addressed Avon as 'Master' and others as 'Sir' or 'Madam'. Slave also apologised continually and was occasionally thrown into panic.

Xena: Warrior Princess

Xena (or *XWP* to the cognoscenti) aired from 1995 to 2001, and was a spin-off from *Hercules: The Legendary Journeys*. Set in a fantastical Ancient Greece that some viewers took for reality, former *Hercules* villain Xena, played by Lucy Lawless, is a steel-thighed, tunic-clad Amazon, conveniently on a quest to redeem her past sins. The stories had a compelling melodrama, slapstick and a sexually ambiguous relationship between Xena and her girlish sidekick Gabrielle (Renee O'Connor). The show featured a wide cast of recurring characters, such as Ares, the god of war, who amid the fetishistic, flashing swordplay and fast-edit fighting somehow managed to be more mythological archetypes than sexual stereotypes. *XWP* has been enthusiastically embraced by lesbian fans, who love the heroine's kickass attitude, her spectacular build and the unmistakable lesbian subtext in her relationship with her sidekick.

The League of Gentlemen
One episode in particular of Mark Gatiss, Reece Shearsmith and Steve Pemberton's cult TV sitcom, 'The Medusa Touch', featured a visit to Royston Vaysey's curious bed-and-breakfast by 'Daddy' and his Heath Robinson-ish erotic breath-control machine Medusa. It's worth seeing, not just because it features Byronic television decorator Laurence Llewelyn-Bowen being hit by a van. Daddy's inflation-suited acolytes are straight out of unsexy British suburbia, but sympathetically portrayed. The creepy, speech-impeded Daddy is reminiscent of an older, check-jacketed, polo-necked master you might find in any town's SM scene. Meanwhile, the dominated bed-and-breakfast owner, and the illicit passion for gardening that he shares with the checkout girl at his local garden centre, has all the danger of dramatic, transgressive passion while the rubber ducks are bland and safe, steaming up their rubber goggles in flock-walled living rooms. The show smacks of pervy inside knowledge on the part of this bizarre comedy team.

Tipping the Velvet
Featuring Diana Rigg's daughter and broadcast by the BBC in 2003, *Tipping the Velvet* (colloquial for cunnilingus), an adaptation of Sarah Waters' novel, brought the lush production values normally associated with costume-drama stories of manners to the melodramatic secret history of 1890s lesbian London. How far this is a historically accurate or a created world is not the point – the novel

itself doesn't pretend to be other than imaginative. Merchant/Ivory meets elements of Sacher-Masoch in the upstairs-downstairs submission games, the fetishistic sense of cheekiness and the cross-dressing (in very fetching scarlet bellhop-style uniform), as lesbian foundling Nan Astley grows as a woman.

FETISH ICON: BATMAN

(fetishes: big rubber cape/masked apprentice)

'Born' in 1939, the Dark Knight, or The Caped Crusader, was created by Bob Kane and Bill Finger for DC Comics. Since his inception, his myth has spawned innumerable versions and references in films, graphic novels and cartoon shows, from the dark visions of Tim Burton's 1989 movie *Batman* to the camp of 1960s TV or Andy Warhol's *Batman Dracula* (1964). Batman cast his shadow at the inception of goth subculture in the 1980s, fitting right in with the cobwebs of the Bat Cave or Slimelight and the comic-strip psychobilly of bands like The Guanabatz, while rubber costumes similar to Michelle Pfeiffer's Catwoman outfit were ubiquitous in magazine spreads: the acceptable face of female fetish in the early 1990s.

The character was inspired by a number of fetishistic associations, including Zorro, The Shadow and Dracula. Batman has always been an unusually grim superhero. Driven by vengeance, in a frightening costume, he is stark and cold next to characters like Superman. The grimness is not a constant; in some incarnations of the character it evaporates into camp and even comedy. In fact, during the 1950s, when the popularity of superhero comics had declined considerably, Batman even acquired a crime-fighting Batdog mascot and an annoying extra-dimensional imp named 'Batmite'.

In his book *Seduction of the Innocent* (1953), psychologist Frederic Wertham used Batman and Robin to attack the comic-book medium. He insinuated that Batman and Robin had a sexual relationship, and asserted that the bare legs in Robin's costume encouraged homosexuality. He succeeded in raising a public outcry, eventually leading to the establishment of the Comics Code Authority. Such fanatically prurient, politically opportunistic opinions earned you cheques in the 1950s America of the anticommunist senator Joseph McCarthy and of the Hays Commission, which famously insisted that one of each actor's feet remained on the floor during Hollywood's bedroom love scenes.

DC Comics returned Batman to his sinister, urban, film-noir roots in the late 1950s, giving rise to the character that most fans are familiar with. For the next 25 years Batman was the mysterious dark avenger of the night, though the popularity of the *Batman* TV series of the 1960s overshadowed the comic books considerably.

Writer Frank Miller further grounded Batman firmly in these grim and gritty origins with the comic book mini-series *The Dark Knight Returns* (1986), which gave a shot in the arm to the entire mainstream comic book industry, as its popularity was nothing short of phenomenal. It allowed Batman to shed his clownish image, and helped to raise the standing of comic books so that they were no longer thought of solely as children's entertainment.

In most versions of the Batman myth, he is the alter ego of Bruce Wayne, a millionaire industrialist who is driven to fight crime after his parents are murdered by a mugger when he is a child. To that end, he spends his youth learning martial arts, criminology, forensics and disguise, among other relevant skills. He wears his bat costume because he believes that criminals are a superstitious lot, and easily scared.

To the world at large, Bruce Wayne appears a superficial playboy. He is known for his contributions to charity, notably through the Wayne Foundation, a charitable body devoted to helping the victims of crime and preventing people from turning to it.

Occasionally, a villain will be struck by the idea that Bruce Wayne is Batman, only to dismiss the possibility because Wayne clearly doesn't have the brains or the nerve to be Batman. He guards his secret so well that his true identity is known only to a handful of individuals, including – wouldn't you know it – Superman. The mind boggles at these superheroes inhabiting the same fictional universe. The superhero support group can only be a few issues away.

Batman's Gotham City is a fictional New York City. He operates from the Bat Cave, a cavern located beneath Bruce Wayne's manor which contains his vehicles, crime lab, gym and computers, together with the redoubtable butler Alfred Pennyworth. Pennyworth was the original model for any number of clichéd British butlers who brush the dust discreetly from their jacket after a fight. Batman's array of equipment is dark, gothic, and bat-styled, from the fetishistic fins of the Batmobile to the decisive throwing-weapon the batarang. Only in the campest versions of the Batman story, however, would the Caped Crusader himself resort to using the bat-prefix. Shamefully, in the 1960s TV series the bat-arsenal included a bat-computer, bat-rope, bat-scanner, bat-radar, bat-cuffs, even a bat-phone.

In heavier versions, Batman keeps most of his personal field equipment in a signature piece of apparel, a yellow utility belt. It typically contains items such as smoke bombs, batarangs, fingerprint kit, a cutting tool, explosives, a grappling-hook gun and a breathing device. As a rule, Batman has an aversion to carrying a firearm (it being the method of his parents' execution), though some stories forgo this plot element and others let him make an exception to this rule by arming his vehicles. He is typically portrayed as a brilliant tactician and detective, but flawed by a humourless personality and an obsession with seeking justice.

As well as having an arsenal of gadgets and weapons, Batman is also a brilliant detective, criminal scientist, tactician and commander. Rather than out-fight his foes, he outwits them. His detective skills put him on a par with Sherlock Holmes. Aside from sidekicks Pennyworth and teenager Robin, the Boy Wonder (who grew into Nightwing in the DC story-line), Batman's famous for his uniquely twisted gallery of rogues. The Joker, the Penguin and the Riddler are out to make Gotham feel their pain. Two-face, meanwhile, is a former District Attorney whose multiple-personality disorder took full hold of him when one side of his face was horribly scarred. He is obsessed with committing crimes with themes of duality and opposites, and all his major decisions are determined by a two-headed coin.

Robin, although present in Batman's life as long ago as 1940, only a year after Batman's creation, is nonetheless the most risible element, presenting the greatest opportunity for camp, especially in the 1960s TV series that starred Adam West as Batman and Burt Ward as Robin. Though it may be tragic, it is nonetheless true that most thirtysomethings would have been introduced to Batman through reruns of this series. Amusingly, in late 1989, DC Comics polled *Batman* readers on whether to kill off the second Robin, Jason Todd. They voted yes, and Todd was subsequently murdered by the Joker.

In the darker stories, Batman battles conventional gangsters, alongside other grizzly villains such as Mr Freeze, Poison Ivy, the shapeshifting Clayface and the Scarecrow. Batman, and Bruce Wayne, square off against Catwoman, in a love–hate dynamic of sexual tension, while Batgirl, introduced in the 1960s, was rendered paraplegic by the Joker and reinvented herself as a research assistant for superheroes.

Batman is not just fetishistic on account of his feline opponents, caped crusading and bat-references. He has the deep flaws of a noir hero – he is obsessed with crime-fighting, all work and no play despite his wealth and pleasures – and it's self-discipline that really drives him. Perhaps the most important part of the Batman myth is that, unlike Superman or the majority of the DC stable, he does not possess any superhuman abilities. Not for him the leaps and bounds of special powers. He is a normal human who has elevated himself to near-superhuman status through discipline and training. He fights with martial arts, high-tech gadgets, custom-designed vehicles, esoteric weapons, brilliant detective skills and a well-trained mind.

4: DIFFERENT STROKES – FETISH AS AN ART FORM

DISCIPLINED DESIGN

Fenders, Speakers and Underwired Bras

Take one look at the world around us, and it's clear that sexually arousing shapes permeate the world of design. The phallic qualities of lipsticks, for example, have been remarked on by the likes of Desmond Morris and Marshall McLuhan. Millionaire magnate, playboy and recluse Howard Hughes, designer of the curvaceous Spruce Goose flying boat, was also a keen brassière designer, bringing an aeronautical, aerodynamic flair to his rather cumbersome creations. Here are a few designs that epitomise the suggestion of sexiness with style:

- Introduced to America in 1955, General Motors' Aerotrain is an anorak's vision of loveliness. Styled to be sleek and streamlined, it was intended to charge across America as optimistic new rolling stock that epitomised the 'jet age'. To that end, it looked, pleasingly, like a very large silver car with a driver's observation bubble on top and a windowless nose like a jet's. It even had tail-fins on its caboose. Unfortunately, it didn't perform as well as it looked, and was out of service within a decade. But it remains the sexiest thing on rails.

- The B & W Blue Boom loudspeaker is just the thing for playing Puccini's *La Bohème* through. It's sleazy, curvaceous, feminine decadence in speaker form, with a design like a woman's body. Surreal fetish-clothing manufacturers E-Garbs made a limited-edition ribbed leather corset for it in the late 1990s, and they are objects from which it is hard to look away.

- Gibson 1958 Les Paul: incorporating masculine and feminine shapes in design harmony, the electric guitar has always been a sexual object, and the Les Paul has been the epitome of sex, most classically as wielded by Jimmy Page in the early 1970s. The Les Paul is a particularly classy guitar, made from mahogany, with a body arched like a violin. Orchestral string sections have always suggested sex too, but in a more receptive, feminine way.

- Art Nouveau: the flowing lines of architects from Gaudi to Mucha seem to melt, drip and pool themselves around doors and windows. This liquefaction of straight lines brings sexual form to practical function, and has dotted the world – including the ironwork at the street entrances of the Paris Metro.

CARS: FROM A BUICK 6

Sex as a design influence, however, is perhaps most apparent in vehicles from the heyday of classic car design. Cars are a good example of the process, active in fetish style, by which one person's prosaic life-detail becomes exotic to someone from another time and place. We can be sure, for example, that an average number of miserable times would have taken place in now classic 1957 Chevrolets during the late 1950s and early 1960s. Today, car design is function-determined, reflecting our view that the car is a necessary evil as much as something to be proud of. But cars were once a liberation, their design all form and expression. They were made to look good in motion, or to have character: a 1954 Buick Special, for example, has a radiator grill not unlike the mouth of an angel fish.

What follows is a subjective top five of the most fetish-friendly cars.

5. Jaguar E-Type: whether firing on six or twelve cylinders, this 1960s thoroughbred is simply a penis on wheels.

4. Chevrolet Corvette Mark II Stingray: the curves of the Mark II 'Vette are simply the most sweeping, waisted and sexy of any car ever. Unlike other Ford and Mopar muscle cars such as the

Mustang and Camaro, or the Dodge Challenger much loved by *The Dukes of Hazzard*, the Stingray had a whiff of futurism about it; a model for those slick, high-tech coupes which culminate with the likes of *Nightrider*.

3. Ford Capri: despite its reputation as the pre-eminent British lads' ride of the 1970s and 1980s, and the working-class muscle car, those sweeping curves were mostly style over content: in all but the three-litre versions, you could walk around the engine with room to spare.

2. 1962 Ford Thunderbird: this incarnation of the famous T-Bird set the tone for a level of high-tech design – swing-away steering wheel, cruise control – that is still state-of-the-art. More importantly, however, the car was designed to look good in motion. Its cigar shape is the epitome of sexy smoothness. Like the Buick Riviera of the same period, it combines high-tech futurism and muscle-car power with a feminine elegance.

1. The Batmobile: Batman's ride in the 1960s TV series was built on a 1955 Lincoln Futura. Exaggerating every fetishistic fin from 1950s 'jet age' car design as if to form a metallic black cape similar to the Caped Crusader's itself, the Batmobile has to be the ultimate fetish vehicle.

MASTERS AND MISTRESSES OF ART

Aubrey Beardsley (1872–1898)

Famously a member of the same set of Chelsea aesthetes as Oscar Wilde, Beardsley's life was all too neatly trimmed. Facing an untimely death, he desired *Venus and Tannhäuser*, his flippant, sensuous illustrated work of erotica, to be destroyed, seemingly aware that art and literary history would view such works as fripperies, footnotes. He hadn't had the opportunity to produce the weightier work of which he felt capable.

Venus and Tannhäuser contains a series of genuinely saturnalian illustrations, heavily drawn, and the text has a precision that implies he could have developed into the artist and writer he so wanted to be. Perhaps he needn't have worried. His rehabilitation, which began with the unwelcome press attention generated by an attempt to ban a London exhibition in the late 1960s, is now complete. In *Venus*, he takes a conspiratorial tone with the reader, inviting you into his created world of delights. His parade of satyrs and unicorns is extreme, bestial, surreal sexual fantasy. Even when they're doing nothing more than waiting on Venus and Tannhäuser with salvers of asparagus, one is always left aware of their sexual potency. Genitals are always on display, swelling not to be ignored, or else readily available to a satyr's finger. The illustrated novella is suffused with a tender eroticism, always with the twist of cruelty that betrays an understanding that passion is often most satisfyingly expressed with precision, the devil in the detail.

Venus and Tannhäuser is permeated with the ripe and rank fruits of a genuinely filthy mind. Mincingly powerful, Beardsley's work, sadly unfinished at the time of his death (it runs to around eighty typeset pages), speaks softly, but carries a big stick.

Hans Bellmer (1902–1975)

A forerunner of Jake and Dinos Chapman, German surrealist Bellmer specialised in creating life-sized distorted or dismembered pubescent dolls – twisted forms placed in empty rooms on wooden floors. His disquieting erotomania led one critic, Sue Taylor, to analyse Bellmer as having a repressed homoerotic attachment to his father, whom he despised with a shivering passion. Not the automatic assumption one would make from a casual glance of his work, but certainly Bellmer's fetishistic vision is so extreme that we suspect family visits to the parents may have been a little strained.

Gene Bilbrew (1923–1974)
A fetish illustrator, he had drawings published in *Exotique* magazine in the late 1950s. He drew under a range of pseudonyms, most famously ENEG.

Robert K. Bishop (1945–1991)
An American bondage artist, he has been compared with John Willie and published extensively in bondage magazines.

H.R. Geiger (b. 1949)
Hans Rudi Geiger is a Swiss painter best known for his work on *Alien* (see pp. 119–20). His heritage goes back further, however. A friend of Salvador Dali and Timothy Leary, he has painted his nightmarish airbrush-work for forty years. More fetishistic than the fantasy art of Boris Vallejo or Frank Frazetta, it's similarly unreal. His painting for the cover of the 1979 Dead Kennedys album *Frankenchrist* was seized by the FBI who, during those hard-ass Reagan years, were out to nail lead singer and Bay Area situationist Jello Biafra with an obscenity lawsuit. As a sculptor, Geiger became interested in interfacing the body with his work, producing furniture such as the Harkonnen Capo Chair, as his fetishistic influences took him towards biomechanics, futureshock and cyberpunk style.

Allen Jones (b. 1937)
Throughout the 1960s and 1970s, Allen Jones turned forbidden sexual desires into art that hung on the walls of the Tate Gallery. A leading light in the Pop Art movement, Jones explored obsessions with nylon, high heels, mannequins and shiny, figure-hugging latex. It was his friend David Hockney who initially pointed out the similarity between his hermaphroditic paintings and 1950s fetish art. This spurred Jones to explore the work of Eric Stanton and his peers such as Gene Bilbrew, which influenced Jones's pictures such as his TV transformation triptych 'Maid To Order I, II, III'. Jones is

similarly famous for his coffee-table sculptures featuring women on all fours. These mannequin-style installations are themselves often parodied in fetish art, and are a powerful and degrading form of objectification which encouraged feminist opprobrium when displayed in 1969. They continue to provide inspiration for fetish furniture and clothing design.

Once one gets through defending Jones's pieces as works of the imagination, however, one then wonders what his art is for. The minimal statements of Pop Art do not perhaps sit well with the powerful emotions of arousal. Although sexual objectification is the point, it's still the case that the concepts wear the women, and rather blandly. Those first-generation feminists had a point about the objectification of women in Jones's case, and it's exactly the point that a sexual sadist would make too: in a sense, those women don't suffer *enough*. While it's fine for Magritte to play conceptual games with us – *c'est ci n'est pas une pipe* – it's not clear what Jones is trying to do with a similar style: *c'est ci n'est pas une femme*? There's none of the eroticism of so horny a 'vanilla' painter as Modigliani: you can have eroticism without fetishism, but do we really need fetish art without eroticism, even in its darkest forms?

Stanton remained furious that Jones used his work for inspiration as he did, and he did it with a certain lack of the powerful psychological content the subject of sadomasochism deserves. Jones's work has something of the sense of the art-world slumming it – which is all well and good until you look back from a point in cultural history, such as now, when the pulp from the gutter looks more worthy than the critical stars.

Gustave Moreau (1826–1898)
This great master of the symbolist era painted images drenched in richness and tainted by indolence. J.K. Huysmans referred to his work as 'disquieting and sinister allegories'. Certainly he chose as his favourite subject mythical females whom it would be unwise to

upset, like Salome or Morgan le Fay. He festooned them with heavy jewels and a sense of malevolence, turning Biblical characters into *femmes fatales par excellence*. Yet he also lent a sense of debauched languidness to his subjects, and imbued all his works with a sense of *fin de siècle* decadence. Whilst his women are mostly powerful, sinister creatures who hold the whip hand, his men are androgynous, effeminate creatures who swoon in their presence.

Felicien Rops (1833–1898)

Anyone who conjures the image of a leather-booted mistress walking her pet pig on a leash has to be worth further investigation. Born in Namur, Belgium, Rops first won fame as a caricature artist and went on to illustrate poetic works for authors including Mallarmé and Baudelaire. He delighted in blending the themes of sex, sacrilege, death and Satanism, the pinnacle of this fusion surely being realised in the gleefully blasphemous painting 'The Temptation of St Anthony', where a voluptuous naked woman replaced Jesus on the cross to torment the horrified saint. Critics in 1868 noted he was 'truly eloquent in depicting the cruel aspect of contemporary woman'. Yet close investigation of Rops' work reveals that his symbolic use of the decadent woman is more a dig at the repressive religion that lusts after her then scorns her. His work played with the power of sexuality almost a century before the surrealists. He seemed to enjoy tweaking the nose of authority and lived a comfortable and happy life.

Sardax

Sardax, the acclaimed SM artist, is in his forties and lives in London. He has worked for *Leg Show*, an American magazine aimed at leg and foot fetishists, and has illustrated many female-dom books. Sardax is most famous for his heavy line-drawings and watercolour paintings that show in their attention to detail that he is enslaved by the mannered, imperious women he draws, who have something of both history and fantasy about them.

Hajime Sorayama (b. 1947)

A Japanese illustrator, his style is typically more realistic than anime and manga, but his subjects aren't: sexy robot women, cyborgs and various sexual meldings of human, machine and animal – the imaginative possibilities are endless.

Eric Stanton (1926–1999)

The colour illustrations of Eric Stanton (born Ernest Stanzoni) appeared in a number of fetish magazines in America from the late 1950s onwards. He's most famous for his lively strips of dominated men, angry women, bondage and humiliation, now readily available in coffee-table collections. Usually following a formulaic pulp-crime plot, some cad, wretch, hapless pageboy-thief or similar figure is bound, humiliated and beaten by way of moral redress. Often Stanton's miscreant's sins are shamefully sexual, the figures popular archetypes of American life – the wimp and the cheerleader, for example: 'I caught him peeking, Ma!' In the sheer exuberance of his work, Stanton set the tone for comic-strip fetish art.

Franco Saudelli (b. 1952)

Saudelli is an erotic comic-book artist whose drawings are typically bondage-filled, melodramatic tales of the tribulations of Italian babes.

Tom of Finland (1920–1991)

Born Touko Laaksonen, Tom of Finland served in World War II before working in advertising in Helsinki. He submitted his drawings to American bodybuilding magazines such as *Physique Pictorial*, which formed a codified gay underground in the conservative 1950s. Tom of Finland's leatherbound muscle-men, bikers, greasy mechanics and sleazy cowboys became key icons in the 1970s leather scene, and his work is much exhibited and copied on greeting cards. In 1979, the Tom of Finland Foundation was formed, a non-profit organisation which preserves and catalogues erotic art. He died of emphysema, but not before having his portrait taken by Robert Mapplethorpe.

John Willie (1902–1962)

John Coutts, better known as John Willie, was a pioneering fetish photographer and bondage artist in the post-war years. Willie was a globetrotter, which is perhaps why his work makes sense to both Brits – especially his 'Sweet Gwendoline' strips – and Americans, through his studio rope-bondage photographs in *Bizarre* magazine. Born in Singapore, educated in England and resident in Australia before moving to New York during World War II, Willie influenced Stanton, Irving Klaw, ENEG, Hanna-Barbera and a host of modern fetish clothing designers. Sadly, when he was diagnosed with a fatal illness in 1961, he wound up his mail-order business and returned to England, destroying his archive in the process.

FETISH PHOTOGRAPHY

Fetish photography has been with us ever since the 1920s, when the surrealist eye was put to the lens. The economics of early photography dictated that the market among the middle classes was for family portraits, while prints of Edwardian curiosa – those evocative images of cheeky, bloomer-clad girls-next-door from another time – were a monied collectors' interest, then as now. Although now we would view them as period fetish, then they were the pornography of the everyday. Photographic erotica became affordable when handy pocket photosets were produced for soldiers as early as World War I. By the end of World War II, servicemen were used to the concept of titillating magazines, which progressed to semi-nudity in the 1950s and then to our modern idea of pornography.

Fetish photography may of course be starkly gynaecological, but its more common tendency is to leave something to the imagination. Influential mainstream art/erotic photographers include Edward Weston, whose black-and-white prints and still-lifes draw out the evocative similarity of all surfaces, whether it's his wife's skin or the skin of a green pepper. Many fetish photographers would claim to do the same thing with kinky second skins.

Little is known about the history of much fetish photography – the picture-takers and models tended to get paid and anonymously go away – although fetish photography as art was delved into by notable masters including Man Ray and Henri Cartier Bresson. The Kinsey Institute has a marvellous collection. Some of them are 'action shots' of couples, showing submission and domination games. Alongside the fetish detail that was intended are some anachronistic period details that raise a smile for the modern viewer: if your life is incomplete without a picture of a young man from the 1930s, Brylcreemed hair framing teeth and lips that grip a horsewhip, then this is the resource.

Saddle Up!
Helmut Newton was the first fashion and nude photographer to incorporate sadomasochistic themes into his work, which he did with elegance and sophistication, and his picture of a model with a saddle on her back, posing on all fours on a bed, is much copied. It's beyond the scope of this book to argue whether such pictures are fine art, erotica, pornography or any combination of these: fetish photography ranges from the sinister necro images of Helmut Wollech to arguably any fashion spread that features a bit of rubber. In the 1980s, Linda Evangelista, Claudia Schiffer and Diane Brill were in particular demand to model the rehabilitated biker chic of the time, and the rubber of designers such as Thierry Mugler. When asked by *Vogue* if rubber dresses demeaned or objectified women, Naomi Campbell replied succinctly, 'Women can wear whatever they like.'

Robert Mapplethorpe (1946–1989)
Mapplethorpe's erotic SM images, which drew their subjects from the photographer's own friends on New York's gay leather scene,

caused much agitation about public funding of the arts. He was hardly as single-interest in his work as in his sexuality, however. He photographed female beauty exceptionally too, and reflected all the diverse tastes of the fetish scene as a whole. He is also famous for his still-life work. Mapplethorpe's point was that to see such fine speci-mens of humanity as he photographed properly, we should see them not only in pornography but well-framed, in gallery spaces, dis-played as well as one would display Michelangelo's 'David', since that's porn too, of the highest order. It's actually a shame that he was interpreted as trying to shock, although he courted that PR too. That almost reduces his work back to porn, instead of the sincere, opti-mistic celebration of humanity and sexuality that it really is.

Fetish Photography Now

In the 1980s it was natural that the fashions of the fetish scene, both leather and rubber, should inspire self-identified fetish photographers to experiment with the reflections of these newly emergent second skins, since playing with light is what photogra-phy is anyway. Much of this work, invariably in black and white by artists such as Trevor Watson and Bob Carlos Clarke, portrays beautiful models in oil-like pools of rubber, and is what many think of as fetish photography. But recent years have seen a revolt into colour and lyricism in fetish pictures, just as they have in fetish fashions. This has also incorporated hitherto more marginal and everyday fetishes, such as the upskirt and stocking pictures of Elmer Batters. The lush, cheesecake-influenced burlesque work of Tim Westwood, reminiscent of Bunny Yaeger's, is typical of this trend, in which location – the sleazy motel room, the naughty nurse's clinic – is everything, and fashions are not just the separatist fetishwear you might expect but the swimsuits and polka-dots of burlesque, or the sophisticated smalls of Agent Provocateur.

Meanwhile, the staples of rubber and leather remain, but are colourful, while pictures that feature fetish paraphernalia have cut the chase with greater explicitness, featuring edge-play, body-modification or even bloodletting. While the 1980s and 1990s SM photography of Della Grace and Housk Randall set the tone of its times in being situational, today's pictures are often more extreme. Richard Kern's pictures, though colourful, are nonetheless sinisterly suggestive and explicit at the same time. With some integrity, Kern doesn't claim to be an artist, but a decent pornographer: 'Porn is not art, because it has a function. Many people will tell you that they find porn boring, repetitive and rather pathetic, actually. These people have obviously been watching bad porn.'

German photographer Helmut Wollech, on the other hand, attracted police attention during the 1990s after the publication of his book *Corpus Subtile*. His necrophilic pictures were so good that they were taken to be real, and one hopes he would claim to be art. They are like police-file photos: the grainy, semi-industrial images are processed in such a way that blotches and scars seem to appear on the flesh of his models. This is dark stuff which reinforces the essential nature of creative freedom. 'If I couldn't take these,' his pictures seem to say, 'I might be creating these scenes for real.'

There is, however, a vibrant internet-based stream of fetish photography in which the model is the star. We all know that most internet porn consists of crass, pop-up-ridden subscription websites that throw in every demeaning porn cliché from the American college jock's Spring Break. Though occasionally there's some humour, a run of anonymous, objectified cum-sucking teens abound. In contrast to this, websites run by fetish models such as Gwendoline, Dita or Bianca are explicit, at least on their subscription pages, imaginative, and draw on the history of fetish art by featuring photo-spread styles and references to fetish characters and fantasy figures. Produced entirely for arousal and to provide a living, they represent an emergent kind of cyber-pulp, part-art, part-porn, that will last as long as there is a market. Meanwhile, the

Sun's photographer Dave Hogan has taken portraits of club-goers at recent *Skin Two* Rubber Ball events – a big change from the days when the only way you'd get a tabloid snapper at a fetish club was to run a secret exposé.

A by no means exclusive list of some other fetish photographers worth an internet search:

• Emma Delves-Broughton

• Wolfgang Eichler

• Steve Diet Goedde

• Doris Kloster

• Christophe Mourthé

• Dave Naz

• Johann Ohngemach

• Martin Perrault

• Doralba Picerno

• Suze Randall

• James Stafford

FETISH ICON: MAN RAY (1890–1976)

(fetishes: the feminine, wrapping, mummification)

Unconcerned, but not Indifferent (Man Ray's epitaph, Montparnasse Cemetery)

Born Emmanuel Radnitzky in Philadelphia, painter, object-maker, avante-garde film maker, Man Ray is best known as a surrealist photographer, producing his first significant photographs in 1918. Living in New York, he formed the American branch of the Dada movement with his close friend Marcel Duchamp. Dada was a radical rejection of traditional aesthetic standards. World War I in particular had led to a cultural distrust in Europe – all received ideas were up for question if the patriotic values that had once seemed indisputable had led to the slaughter of a generation. Americans, traditionally more upbeat than war-ravaged Europe, nonetheless adopted the absurdist theme of this message: art predicated on the understanding that the world is, at least, absolutely barking mad.

Likewise, Dadaism defined itself in terms of traditional art – it could not blaspheme against 'high' art without referring to it. Incorporating lettering into a painting for example, like Braque, is not shocking now in the way it was in the 1920s, before it became part of the artistic vocabulary. The Surrealist and Dadaist ideas cross-pollinated, and, if there's a difference between Surrealism and Dada, then Surrealism is less a comment on history or art that has gone before and more a pure, rank fruit of the imagination.

Culture had concerned itself with imagination before – from the Romantics through the visions of early fantastical horror writers like LeFanu and Poe. (Surrealists themselves claimed inspiration from alchemy, Dante, Bosch, Sade, Lautréamont and Rimbaud.) But Surrealists did imagination without the egotism of the Romantics; in fact, they believed quite the opposite – that art could be 'pure psychic automatism' (André Breton, *The Surrealist Revolution*, 1924), automatism being spontaneous creative production without conscious moral or aesthetic self-censorship. Man Ray's work shows how this definition could be broadened to incorporate a fetish and fashion sensibility.

Real Surreal

In 1920, Man Ray stated that 'Dada cannot live in New York,' and flounced off to live and work in the Montparnasse quarter of Paris during an era of great creativity and sexual experimentation. It was there that he fell in love with the famous French singer, model, painter and muse Kiki, or Alice Prin, who was the epitome of bohemian Paris, so much so that her memoirs remained banned in the USA until the 1970s.

Kiki modelled many of Man Ray's conceptions of womanhood, while the famous American socialite, war photographer and feminist icon Lee Miller lived and worked with Man Ray. As his favoured model between 1929 and 1932, Miller was transformed into both fashion inspiration and surrealist fetish.

With Max Ernst, Jean Arp, André Masson, Pablo Picasso and Joan Miró, Man Ray was shown at the first Surrealist exhibition at the Galerie Pierre in Paris in 1925. For the next twenty years in Montparnasse, he revolutionised the art of photography. Artists of the day such as James Joyce and Jean Cocteau posed for his camera. In 1934, Merét Oppenheim (she of the furry cup and saucer) posed for Man Ray in what has become a very well-known series of photographs depicting the Surrealist artist nude, standing next to a printing press.

A fashion photographer for *Vogue* and *Harpers Bazaar*, Man Ray, with his eroticism and optical games, made a lasting mark on the image of modern art, as evident, for example, in his famed work 'Violon d'Ingres' (1924), in which Kiki's body is transformed into the body of a violin, with two f-holes in the small of her back. Her neck joins her nape as a violin's neck joins its headstock, as she turns her face over her shoulder to the viewer.

No Strings Attached

Man Ray experimented tirelessly with new photographic techniques – multiple exposure, 'Rayographs' and solarisation were some of his most famous creations, although Lee Miller certainly had a hand in the latter. He played with shadows and light: banisters, sinister in their stillness, cast a dark spiral. Similarly, silks, flesh and hair wind languorously around his pictures, seen in new ways: strange, striking images that transform our perceptions of reality.

Many of his pictures move away from visual resemblance and into the realm of puns and allusions: taking the above example, Ingres was a keen but by all accounts insufferable amateur violinist, and *violon d'Ingres* refers to an artist's folly, on which he spends a disproportionate amount of time compared to his abilities. Did Man Ray think Kiki was his *violon d'Ingres*?

What object, what machine, is more beautiful than a stringed instrument? Man Ray's work is about the feminine as form, about woman as *thing*. With much of his work the viewer is confronted with an object to be unravelled by the understanding, as well as enjoyed. In one work the unwrapping becomes literal: his 'Enigma of Isadore Ducasse' (1920) depicts a lumpy object wrapped in sacking and tied round with rope. He shared this sinister surrealism with collaborators such as André Boiffard: the dark lines of Boiffard's 'Sacs contre sac Amiens' – ghoulish, underexposed pictures of the interior of Amiens Cathedral – make the inside of the church look like the lines of a slender nude. Man Ray's work sometimes shares the curves of Dali and the compelling, sinister quality of André Masson's 'Don Quixote and the Chariot of Death'.

Revolution in the Head

Surrealists were interested in the sensations they created in the viewer. The word 'sensation' has provided art with an important *double entendre*. On the one hand, think of a mannered Edwardian promenade through Paris – Edith Wharton and Henry James, quietly romantic, swap notes on their impressions and sensations. On the other, tabloid newspapers are emblazoned with 'sensational' headlines. The title of Charles Saatchi's Brit-Art exhibition 'Sensation' at the Royal Academy in 1998 alluded to both.

After spending the post-war years in LA, which had become an artists' mecca with the likes of David Hockney and Allen Jones (see p. 89), Man Ray died in 1976. He remains the artistic inspiration of fetish fashion photography, and a fetish touchstone. Not until Helmut Newton were fetish elements quite so explicitly incorporated once more into fashion photography.

Belgian Surrealist Rudolphe Ubach said that in his art he had tried to compare the body with stones. This comparison is a feature of black-and-white photography – British photographer Edward Weston made smooth, pebble-like surfaces out of his wife's curves, for example. The comment could just as well be attributed to Man Ray, except Man Ray's stones are also sculptures! They are fetishistic images fashioned out of nature rather than depictions of the nude itself.

Anyone thinking about feminine elegance in fetish style will think of Man Ray's influence whether they know it or not. There's a fetish night in Cambridge, Massachusetts, called Man Ray, while today's fetish photographers such as Eric Kroll happily acknowledge a Man Ray influence.

5: HOT WAX – THE BEATS AND BREAKS OF BONDAGE

Most music that deals with fetish, it has to be said, is a bit naff. It's as if music comes from a different part of the brain to sexual arousal. And people with pervy tastes who also have good taste in music often don't mix the two. The fetish clubbing experience before trance music could often be a dour, doom-laden affair, with no break from goth. Perhaps it was just as well – anything more exciting could have spurred rubber-clad dancers to lose too much fluid. Fortunately, trance at least gave fetish DJs some records to spin which were atmospheric, but upbeat too, such as is featured on the Torture Garden *Extreme Clubbing* compilations.

Among the less naff options, 'Krautrock' and Kraftwerk-inspired electronica, with its regimented, totalitarian overtones, became popular. These themes were played with by Joy Division and New Order, whose Peter Hook, in particular, associated himself with pervery, especially during his time in Revenge. It's worth distinguishing between music to have fetishistic sex to and music that just sings about it. Gonzo offerings such as The Tubes' 'Mondo Bondage', for example, are social comment and best not mixed with the real thing! Some brave bands, such as The Geni-torturers, have endeavoured over the years to mix the theatricality of Alex Harvey with their music in fetish clubs, which is all well and good, but in that context it's a live sex show, performance rather than rock 'n' roll.

GOTHS AND FETISH

Any Colour so Long as It's Black
Goth used to be a sub-classification of punk. In the early to mid-1980s, it emerged as a subculture in its own right, complete with its own graphic art, literature, music and fashion. There is so much

diversity within global goth culture that its members strongly resist attempts at definition and labelling. And yet, from crushed-velvet, Byronic pretty-boys to industrial, SM and electronic fans, fetishistic music has its own stereotypes.

Goth unashamedly celebrates the dark recesses of the human psyche. Swoon as if from sudden blood-loss, and you're there: dark sensuality, sweeping sadness, morbid fascination, forbidden love, the beauty of enduring pain, and vision before reason. The word 'gothic', with or without a capital 'g', was first used to describe 1980s post-punk bands; bands which were close to the spirit of punk, but with a more despairing, introverted form of anger, and more noodly-sounding keyboards. The first generation of goths, thinly nourished by music journalist Mick Mercer's *Zig Zag* magazine, and nights watching bands like Specimen at the Bat Cave, were wimpy punks who turned their aggression against themselves by speaking the language of mortality, deathly pallor and self-harm partly in order not to frighten their grandmothers with the gobbing inappropriateness of punk behaviour.

Goth subculture can be traced directly back to punk and new wave; to the sexuality of Siouxsie Sioux's thigh-booted *Sturm und Drang* domination and taciturn Robert Smith's The Cure, who began as spiky power-pop and mutated into something more plangent, Smith transforming himself, with black clothes, pancake, lipstick and eyeliner, into a cross between Baudelaire and Baby Jane. Other bands such as Killing Joke, Bauhaus and Sex-Gang Children bravely extolled surrealism and sexual dissipation while wearing string vests in winter, while The Sisters of Mercy provided a scene soundtrack in 'Temple of Love'.

Countless bands began to allude to the geekily gothic. Alien Sex Fiend shared a sense of comic-book horror kitsch with popular psychobilly bands such as King Kurt. Leather trousers crept in amongst the crushed velvet drainpipes and blue suede winklepickers. Gothic bootlace ties put a New Orleans spin on a country and western fashion: goth was crossing the Atlantic.

Global Goths

In the early 1980s, death-rock was on the rise in LA, with such bands as Gun Club, Christian Death, Black Flag, Wall of Voodoo and Skinny Puppy adding sinister to the sunnier lexicon of LA punk bands such as X. Though their music was more like US hardcore than UK goth (which was commonly referred to as 'gothic punk' until at least the mid-1980s), these bands dressed as if they avoided daylight, like denizens of darkened fetish clubs. So far, in America, only The Cramps, with their B-movie sexploitation look, had pioneered a pervy style.

Goth was as much a European phenomenon as it was British or American. Germany spawned such dark and pervy creations as Xmal Deutschland, Die Krupps and Der Mussolini to complement the nascent electronica of Kraftwerk. Throughout the 1980s, there was much cross-pollination between the European goth subcultures, the US death-rock movement and the New Romantics.

The rise in popularity of global rock music in the mid-1980s was mirrored by the rise of gothic rock, most notably in the form of goth rock bands Fields of the Nephilim and The Mission. Australia, via London, produced the dark Lothario heart of Nick Cave and The Birthday Party. South America would produce lurid goth metal bands such as Sepultura. Goth remains both provincial and global. To sophisticated urbanites it'll always be a little too obvious a vehicle, with its broad references to sex and death, with which to demonstrate one's understanding of the finer points of style. And yet there are kids wearing Cure T-shirts in Mexico City, so there must be something cosmopolitan to it!

Deathly Don Juans

Goth has survived other subcultures. Although always pervaded by a whiff of dope smoke, and originally lubricated by an unholy mix of cider and lager, it has never been self-consciously druggy in the way that dance music has been, or the hippies were. Despite its cultural closeness, it never shared the punks' taste for speed, while if you did coke but had a spiky haircut then you were a rich New Romantic, not a goth. Goth's drug of choice – notionally – would have been laudanum. But it never needed one – sex was its drug, and just like drugs it carried its own dissipated, deathly casualties.

It is possible that goth, with its fetish for sex and death, is much more than a modern subculture; that it is a version of a sensibility that has always been a part of humanity. Fascination with all things dark and morbid is nothing new. It may be that the punk scene was a catalyst to give form to a vision that had previously been expressed in the writings of Edgar Allen Poe and Mary Shelley and in Horace Walpole's *The Castle of Otranto*. Some seeds may have been sown in the mid-nineteenth century with the Gothic Revival, and the morbid mood of national mourning at the time of Prince Albert's death.

Over-ripe Fruits

Some say that goth is defined by androgyny, black clothes, black hair dye, heavy make-up, horror, nihilism, sensuality, silver jewellery or any number of other clichés. Others would claim that this just plays into a simple-minded version of unoriginal street style, and that it's based on a more deeply held sensibility of jaded sexuality and the perishability of things. Death is a reason for hedonism – if fruit grows rank and over-ripe, then it should be eaten.

It's no surprise therefore that the barriers between goth and fetish fashion broke down. Soft Cell had mixed bedsit/clubland sleaze with gothic styles and hollow eyes that came both from make-up and dissipation, while Sigue Sigue Sputnik brought explosive fetish-club fashions (lead singer Martin Degville was a fetish market-trader) to the singles chart, even though their musical longevity couldn't be sustained by the two notes in their repertoire.

Although a PVC skirt had been matched with a pair of fishnets since punk, UK goth clubs such as Camden's Full Tilt and Islington's Slimelight began to feature more and more clubgoers in custom-made fetishwear.

Sunglasses after Dark

The 1990s saw the development of goth music in a more industrial-fetish direction, with bands such as Nine Inch Nails and Project Pitchfork bringing a more processed edge to the goth music style. The largely German phenomenon of Darkwave also evolved, with Das Ich at the forefront.

Marilyn M – Superstar

Marilyn Manson is a self-identified goth, and hugely influenced by fetish fashion as well as fascinated by religious imagery and ritual. He goes out with fetish model Dita, and has produced fetishistic videos directed by Chris Cunningham (most famous for his scary images of Aphex Twin). Although it's heresy to call him a goth in some black-clad circles, his music owes a lot to original British goth bands such as The Sisters of Mercy, even though the social comment is very un-goth and owes more to the gonzo-fetish of much-costumed, semi-theatrical bands such as Slipknot.

High-School Geekdom

Whereas the early goth bands that came out of punk would have been keen to avoid labels, performers today proclaim themselves goths and speak for high-school geeks, rather than pondering the hereafter. Goth continues to evolve in the twenty-first century, embracing influences from dance culture and anime, but has always retained one thing in common with fetish culture: you can't maintain an atmosphere of despair for very long without someone laughing, and goths, since the 1980s, have delighted in self-parody.

IGGY POP

When Rents talks to the schoolgirl Diane about his love of Iggy Pop in Irvine Welsh's *Trainspotting*, she assumes he's dead. And that was written in the early 1990s. First as notorious frontman of The Stooges in the late 1960s, Iggy Pop has shared his craven sexual longing, pain – and longing for pain – with the public for around 35 years. It's been a long time since he quenched his fire onstage and gouged his chest with the broken bottle. Like the Velvets, he's been appreciated retrospectively, and has therefore been most famous when working least. Though it doesn't sound much different from a Glitter-Band stomp now, 'I Wanna Be Your Dog' remains a masochistic anthem despite the serial attempts of bad covers bands to murder it, and the Bowie-inspired *Lust for Life* album still captures lost souls and urban sleaze with the kind of fascination that thinks it's untouchable because it's half polluted itself. Iggy Pop has a voice like a torch singer who got burnt.

SOFT CELL

Former art students Marc Almond and Dave Ball gave the early 1980s a huge injection of sleaze with their chart-topping pervy synth pop and fab first album *Non-Stop Erotic Cabaret*. The album was a huge hit, despite its celebrating a twilight world of aberrant sexuality and red-light, low-lifestyle living. Their brand of electro-deviance found an enthusiastic audience, from lonely lovers in the Bedsit Land of which they sang to teenaged girls who embraced their pseudo-goth look, sporting accessories like three-row studded metal belts and lacy fingerless gloves. How many teenage bedrooms must have resounded to songs like 'Say Hello, Wave Goodbye', which made the top five, and 'Sex Dwarf', with its memorable chorus 'Isn't it nice/Sugar and spice/Luring disco dollies to a life of vice?' Even the decadent duo's vanilla torch-songs – such as their chart-topping version of Gloria Jones's 'Tainted Love' – were so bitchily camped up that they evoked a whiff of Weimar Republic Berlin.

MADONNA – HER MADGESTY

It's hard to believe it now of the respectable, not to say disapproving, home-maker and children's author, but Madonna Ciccione, at the height of her pop-fame in the early 1990s, published an innovative, incredibly daring, beautifully produced book of photographic fantasies. It featured her often naked, in a variety of sexual scenes: a New York biker in a bondage loft; a B-movie starlet at an orgy; a Monroe-esque nude; a rope-bound submissive leatherdyke; a prostitute in the hands of a tender old man; in a lesbian clinch with Isabella Rossellini – all lavishly photographed by Steven Meisel.

Madonna had always flirted with contrived pop controversy. Her sneaky, witty song titles and lyrics were always cheekily flirty – 'Like a Virgin' – while her use of religious imagery as jewellery poked fun at the Roman Catholic Church which was her cultural heritage. She needled the church when she could – 'Papa Don't Preach' is a rant against clerical mores – and she was accused by American evangelists of recording backwards satanic messages – 'I love Satan' – into her music during the 1980s.

Not all of her attempts to incorporate her playful, edgy, sluttish sexual drive into her music were successful, of course. While Madonna was put across actor friend Rupert Everett's knee in *The Next Best Thing* (2000), she has also been cinematically chastised in *Swept Away* (2003). Similarly, some of her musical references to fetish have been questionable, especially those associated with Warren Beatty's *Dick Tracy* flop, in which she co-starred. The spanking references in 'Hanky Panky' should be taken in the context of 1940s raincoat-clad pastiche. They may not be great lyrics but it's easy to forget that, at the time, they were brave. Madge's *Sex* (1990) was similarly so. Innovatively packaged by Secker & Warburg in a sealed foil bag and shipped in a very hyped process to bookstores for simultaneous and newsworthy publication, it was a publishing phenomenon that sold out in hours and was seldom reprinted. Many buyers bought a second, collectors' copy, in order to have one to leave unopened. Some bookstores limited buyers to one each. It was hype that worked, and the demand was great.

Madonna took a huge risk with her career – never before had a pop princess appeared naked, let alone been shown indulging her kinky fantasies repeatedly. Incredibly, part of the achievement is that not only did her career survive, but her music got better. She moved through vogueing; through the eyecatching fetishism of Gaultier's conical bras, basques, corsets and suspenders; and through camp cabaret style until, embracing trip hop beats, the material girl got in touch with her wistful side.

Sex, however, established her as a serious contributor to fetish politics. In the early 1990s submissive female fantasies were more often associated with a capitulation to patriarchal values than they are now. Madonna helped to show that submissive female sexuality was in fact a reclaiming of ground for the empowered. The chutzpah and serious import of *Sex* suggest that Madonna, though growing older gracefully with her posh Mockney husband, may surprise us yet.

SOUNDTRACKS: SCHULMÄDCHEN REPORT/VAMPYROS LESBOS/MURDER FOR PLEASURE

Similarly worthwhile from today's burlesque, cheesy, easy and ironic point of view are a couple of film soundtracks. You'd be tempted to think that anything by Gert Wilden and his Orchestra would sound somewhere between James Last and Richard Clayderman. We're not talking cutting-edge here. But *Schulmädchen Report*, a collection of German soft-porn film soundtracks recorded in 1971, is a sleazy but sweet 'n' innocent collection that's much better than it had to be. So much more *Boogie Nights* than 'Boogie Nights'. Meanwhile, cheesy porn horror soundtrack *Vampyros Lesbos*, by various studio bods and available from Motel Records, will make you feel like you're having cruel but sophisticated sex in Cannes in 1970, which is when it was recorded. Who wants to listen to *songs* about kinky sex while you're actually having some? And these make a change from Enigma or Gregorian chant. *Murder for Pleasure* features soundtracks from Euro horror movies of the 1970s, such as Mario Bava's wonderfully schlocky *Five Dolls for an August Moon* – a prime candidate for a languid afternoon of decadence and gin and tonics.

HOT ON THE HEELS OF LOVE

A TOP 5 OF PERVERTED POP

5. Throbbing Gristle/Psychic TV: These two vehicles for the robust electronica of Cosey Fanny Tutti and Genesis P. Orridge were ahead of their time. The couple made sex-music before ambient music, and wore their pervertedness on their uniformed sleeves. Although the sounds are quaint now, Throbbing Gristle had sussed an advantage of synthesisers: that music makes a much better soundtrack for sex when you can't visualise the instruments.

4. Dr Octagon: Serious devotees of medical fetishism looking for a soundtrack to accompany their physical examinations could do worse than hip-hop surrealist Dr Octagon, whose 1996 Mo Wax album *Octagonocologist* is a labyrinthine aural journey through corridors, operating theatres, examination rooms etc., all to tough beats, while the sleeve (as it were) features a severed forearm.

3. Ute Lemper: Jazz and classical singer Ute Lemper has never been a traditional Broadway babe, and her 2000 album *Punishing Kiss*, with guest appearances from Nick Cave, Philip Glass and Neil Hannon, is a defiant, fetishistic and cruel portrait of love in the twenty-first century. Lemper has always loved and recorded the world-weary, booze-soaked satirical songs of Brecht and Weill, and the recordings on this album bring out their qualities of decadent, rank corruption to the full.

2. Pete Burns: A Liverpool contemporary of ˙Echo and the Bunnymen and The Teardrop Explodes. Despite these critic-pleasing beginnings, Burns and his 'band' Dead or Alive gleefully built a career on one hi-NRG hit, 'You Spin Me Round'. Burns presented himself as a fetishistic dominant, half Cruella deVille and half Lily Savage, pulling on his latex gloves at any opportunity.

1. Adam and the Ants: The original line-up of Adam and the Ants was more pervery than piracy. Not yet the dandy highwayman, Adam was a regular in Vivienne Westwood's Sex boutique on Chelsea's King's Road, and celebrated kinky pleasures with a barrow-boy's cheek in songs such as 'Lady' and 'There's a Whip in My Valise'. Rumour has it that Adam once missed an appointment with his record company – he had been waiting in the lobby in a sound-deadening, blindfolding leather hood and face mask, and hadn't heard himself called.

FETISH ICON: THE VELVET UNDERGROUND

Thirty-four years have passed since the breakup of The Velvet Underground, and it's hard to imagine now how little that event mattered to anyone then interested in rock 'n' roll. None of their four studio albums for Polydor – *The Velvet Underground and Nico*, *White Light/White Heat*, *The Velvet Underground* and *Loaded* – had dented the Top 100. The last two records never charted at all. Recordings of the band's shows which followed the departure of John Cale, recorded in modest clubs in cities such as Cleveland and Philadelphia, betray a smattering of handclaps that suggest they were recorded at a midweek 'alternative' night in Northampton, UK, one mid-1980s winter.

Tired, broke and ignored, the Velvets split in August 1970, remembered if at all for their brief period as protégés of pop-art superstar

Andy Warhol. Since then, staying on the critical radar largely thanks to Lou Reed's erratic solo career, which kicked off with the breakthrough hit 'Walk on the Wild Side' in 1972, they have grown to become a touchstone of dark, noisy, soulful, pervy indie music: 1960s-fodder for shoe-gazers who don't buy the rockin' postures of The Beatles, Stones or Doors. Their posthumous rehabilitation began in the early 1980s, when they were cited as an influence by bands such as the Jesus and Mary Chain, and a raft of collegiate rockers who gravitated either to their sardonic songs or to their feedback. By an odd pretzel of historical cause and effect, they even found their name borrowed in Czechoslovakia's Velvet Revolution.

Reed, the group's songwriting engine, had been a student at Syracuse University, an admirer of William Burroughs, Raymond Chandler and – more significantly for a middle-class boy casting around for sleaze in New York City from the safety of home – Hubert Selby Jr. After graduation, Reed worked as an in-house songwriter at Pickwick Records, working nine-to-five, turning emotion into kitsch with pop product such as 'The Ostrich', a variant on The Twist: 'it's gonna knock you dead/when we come upside your head'. John Cale was a viola player with minimalist classical performance group The Dream Syndicate, but nonetheless had hair long enough to pass for a pop musician at Pickwick, too. Cale was apparently initially unimpressed with Reed, until he heard some of the songs, including 'Heroin', that would make it on to the Velvets' first album. Mo Tucker and Sterling Morrison completed the lineup.

The band settled on the name The Velvet Underground after a trashy book by Michael Leigh which was found in a street on the Bowery. The cover copy proclaimed the book 'a documentary on the sexual corruption of our age', which seemed appropriate. In retrospect, the band were clear that the name was a matter of image rather than lifestyle. Sterling Morrison said: 'The name was chosen because it sounded nice and it alluded to the underground scene in cinema. And we had "Venus in Furs" written already. The band never set out to be devoted to sexual weirdness. It was a purely literary exercise.'

Nevertheless, a spirit of sexual subversion – or maybe it's just sleaze, depending on how you rate their looks – suffused the Velvets, both in their subject matter and their performances, from Mo Tucker in rope bondage on early publicity pics, to Warhol buddy Gerard Malanga licking a dominatrix's boots during a live performance of 'Venus in Furs'. As hammy and earnest as this sounds, it hadn't been done in living memory. It's not just in the name, in the neo-European cabaret decadence, in the recycled Hamburg-era Beatles leathers and shades, in featured Warhol starlet Nico's Teutonic imperiousness; or that they wrote 'Venus in Furs', which, in any case, you don't have to be a lobotomised Oasis fan to find pretty self-conscious and literary. It's also in Lou Reed's songs, which are forever making up their mind whether to be ironic or sleazily romantic, and in Cale and Morrison's squalling arrangements. They hung out at Warhol's easy-come, easy-go Factory, and yet they made music for loners: solipsistic songs written to be listened to at five a.m., on your own. To the extent of taking the piss sometimes, the Velvets made music for themselves.

Reed fell in love with Nico, writing 'Femme Fatale', 'I'll Be Your Mirror' and 'All Tomorrow's Parties' for her. But he was cruel to her too, having no desire to see the Velvets become the Factory house band, there to back any starlet Warhol thought could – or couldn't – sing. John Cale had written much of the Velvets' second album including the fetishistic 'The Gift', in which Waldo Jeffers' lovelorn longing for the college sweetheart he imagines being faithless leads him to mail himself to her. But Reed also brought about Cale's departure, in completing their third album. Still, 'artist uses people in his work' isn't exactly a shock headline.

But Warhol understood that, despite their talent, people weren't going to come and see the Velvets on their own. Nico gave them sensation to add to their bourgeois fascination with evil, a reserved subterranean cool that stayed with them, and the glamour to attract New York's beau monde. As Paul Morrissey put it, 'I saw Nico as a modern Marlene Dietrich . . . she didn't jump and scream like Janis Joplin or any of those ugly West Coast hippies.' With Sterling Morrison and Nico dead, and plaudits heaped on the living, it's worth remembering that The Velvet Underground were a team effort. And, for a long time before their influence was felt, if you wanted an alternative to the music that celebrated the provincialism of cruising your High School peers around your local town before settling down and breeding, they were your best bet.

6: KINK ON CELLULOID – FETISH FLICKS

Fetish in the Movies

Cinema has been littered with filmic references to fetish, ever since Louise Brooks turned her slender neck to face the camera in Pabst's *Pandora's Box* in 1929. From the Weimar style of *Cabaret* to the controversial scourgings of Mel Gibson's *The Passion of The Christ*, one could point to a legion of scenes on which you could put a kinky spin, whether they're intended to sexualise their subject or not.

It's a bit literal-minded, however, to chronicle every crack of a whip or turn of a booted ankle, unless you want to end up with a dry list of punishment scenes. Take for example, Just Jaeckin's 1975 version of *The Story of O*: an R-rating has prompted many a perv to anticipate seeing it, only to find themselves trashing time with a piece of 1970s cheese that's not dissimilar to 'erotic thrillers' such as *The Stud*, *The Bitch* or *Emmanuelle*.

On the other hand, you might expect sexploitation spills and thrills from Pasolini's *Salo* (1975), a transposing of Sade's *120 Days of Sodom* to Italy in 1944, but what you have is a profoundly disturbing meditation on the sexual impulse towards fascism that's utterly faithful to the humane if bleak political spirit of Sade, Octave Mirbeau and pre-war anarchism – brutal and anything but a turn-on.

The heroes and villains of silent films themselves inspired a deep vein of comic-book power-play such as John Willie's *Sweet Gwendoline*, and every dastardly fetish villain or helpless moppet, while horror is another genre through which the fingernails of fetish have worked their way into the flesh of the mainstream. From silent-era men-monsters, through Hammer Horror and affectionate pastiches from Polanski, vampires have provided a convenient substitute for the sins of the flesh, being themselves nocturnal and otherworldly creatures, not dissimilar to the public image of perversion. Leaving aside Italian and Spanish lesbian vampire movies, there are a huge number of crossovers between horror and erotic thrillers with decent production values, such as *The Hunger*, or some of the more obscure Euro horror titles that have thankfully found their way onto DVD. However, as the vampire/sex crossover is such a vast area, there isn't the space to do it justice in this small book, and I shall choose to leave the fanged ones for another publication.

Horror also yields bondage images – from the wonderful camp of *The Mask of the Red Death* to the sophomoric suffocations of Clive Barker – which go to prove that fear and terror have always been more acceptable to censors than arousal. This goes for mainstream Hollywood releases too: America needs Baddies, and it's an easy move to pop a pervert in that spot. In 1991's *The Silence of the Lambs*, for example, 'bad' serial killer Buffalo Bill is luridly shown making up as a transvestite. 'Good' serial killer Hannibal Lecter, meanwhile, has interests such as gourmet cooking and not only knows what fava beans are but how long to soak them for, even if he does eat them with human flesh.

Similarly, to sit down with Nicholas Cage and Joachim Phoenix in *Nine Mil* is to wonder when the man who starred in *Wild at Heart* and *Raising Arizona* went so off the mark. This is a film which collapses all sorts of behavioural distinctions, as if to satisfy our prurient tabloid imaginings, and has SMers rubbing shoulders with the producers of snuff films. Control-loss, bondage and sexual terror, when presented as entertainment in mainstream movies, are often part of a similar, silent conspiracy of denial between maker and consumer. But then no one ever got rich by avoiding hypocrisy. The following thirty films, by contrast, display a variety of strange, unexpected and sometimes influential cinematic moments.

THE ALL-TIME TOP 30 FILMS WITH A FETISH TWIST

After Hours (Martin Scorsese, 1985)

A comedy thriller from the master of New York cinema in which yuppie office worker Paul Hackett finds himself stranded in SoHo. It's a bygone, pre-Guiliani Manhattan, peopled by perverts, sado-masochists and irate mobs led by ice-cream vendors. Griffin Dunne's bewildered boy goes in search of coffee with bohemian chicks but has to swallow more than he bargained for, mistakenly freeing submissive Linda Fiorentino from her willing bondage, and finding himself mummified in bandage and plaster of Paris. It's a darker take on an otherwise execrable genre that was spawned in the 1980s, best exemplified by *Something Wild*, of wish-fulfilment films for risk-free young professionals.

Ai No Corrida/In the Realm of the Senses (Nagisa Oshima, 1976)

A penetrating study of sexual obsession and escape from conven-tion, *Ai No Corrida* is a thoughtful film even though it's renowned for its explicit scenes. Made in 1976, the film is set in 1936, as the Japanese population prepares for the coming war. Despite this, the services of geisha girls are in as much demand as they ever were. Sada (Eiko Matsuda) is a new girl under the employ of brothel-keeper Toku (Aio Nakajima). This position is a matter of necessity, rather than choice, for Sada, who's compelled to pay off her bank-rupt husband's debts. The work isn't too insufferable, though, even when an old beggar staggers by in search of a sexual favour.

Sada first comes into contact with Toku's husband Kichi-zo (Tatsuya Fuji) when she takes umbrage at the label of prostitute, though she's already glimpsed Toku ministering to Kichi-zo. Pretty soon he becomes a familiar figure, sneaking up and groping Sada while she's vainly trying to scrub the floor. His sexual appetite is legendary and it doesn't matter, to him, that they're both married. Hence, within a short space of time, Sada allows herself to be drawn into Kichi-zo's bedchamber (he is her master after all) where they engage in a bout of frivolous sex. At this instant their increasingly frequent bouts of fucking are free and easy, full of delicious orgasms.

Gradually their relationship intensifies, each of them finding satisfaction only within their gymnastically physical clinches. Kichi-zo finds that he's somewhat jealous of her clients, even though the money they bring in is useful, so he makes an 'honest' woman of Sada by marrying her. Now their relationship shifts to one of equals. Whenever Sada wants sex, which is often, she demands it. She leads Kichi-zo around by his penis, such is her attachment to his instrument of pleasure. Similarly, Kichi-zo gets the best of both worlds by sleeping with his first wife when he feels like it and returning to Sada at other times. As it intensifies, it's obvious their relationship is on a trajectory that can only go sour.

But this film makes voyeurs of its audience: uniquely in cinema, we are watching the actors come, as lovers, for real. And yet that proves uneasy viewing, because this is sex unmediated by the comforting conventions of porn. Throughout the film, there is barely a moment when sex of some sort isn't taking place, yet it is thoroughly integrated into the story rather than a gratuitous, exploitative addition.

Society gives the impression of being tolerant and permissive, since individuals can reach the heights of ecstasy in full view of their servants, friends and relatives. However, the reality is exactly the opposite. People are in fact so repressed that they'll barely comment on people fucking in front of them, instead pretending that it's just not happening. Meanwhile, the audience becomes numbed by the sheer repetition and increasingly bizarre lewdness of the sex, as SM and erotic asphyxiation enter the picture.

As the lovers' light-hearted dalliance mutates into something altogether darker, the subtle emotional nuances of the characters shift, adjusting to the new balance. Through actions and imagery, the establishment of Kichi-zo's penis as a character in its own right takes place. Sada becomes inseparable from the cock, wishing to hold and caress it, choosing it over Kichi-zo himself, as the envelope of obsession tightens around them.

Ai No Corrida is truly unique in its uncompromising portrayal of insatiable lusts, control and obsession. The characters have sex constantly, like breathing, and continue to live, eat, talk and play musical instruments as they do so. It's not long before any sense of titillation has gone, and the audience is left feeling quite refractory. Inspired by a newspaper story in which a disorientated former geisha was arrested wandering the streets with her lover's severed penis, it's amazing cinema that succeeds in taking you to where love gets dangerous.

Alien (Ridley Scott, 1979)

A genuinely scary and violent SF masterpiece that re-injected terror into the genre, which had become dominated by concept-driven work. 'In Space No One Can Hear You Scream' was the film's tagline. A mining mission picks up an alien hitchhiker after being duped into tracing a distress signal, and ends up with several bloody deaths and one very nasty monster. Aside from the spooky production values, Sigourney Weaver is memorable in her breakthrough performance, as is the alien's first appearance, out of John Hurt's exploding chest. It's punk SF, a return from high-concept, highfalutin ideas to B-movie tension in which the characters are trapped and killed one by one, and was in fact inspired by 1958 movie *It! The Terror from Beyond Space*.

Why it's included here, however, is on account of the designs of Swiss fetish painter Hans Rudi Geiger (see p. 89). Fetish can be about facing our fears. Geiger created a monster which is as popularly memorable as the shark in *Jaws* (and bears about as much relationship to reality), and which reared terrifyingly out of his unconscious to win him an Oscar for Best Visual Effects. Geiger popularised the huge fetish, biomechanical and prosthetic influences in his own work, which in turn fed back into the scene, informing cyber-punk styles too: fetish events such as Torture Garden or the *Skin Two* Rubber Ball have regularly featured dread-locked denizens clad in all manner of industrial rubberised tubing, Hazchem symbols, masks and other phuture-fuck paraphernalia that clearly require the wearer to take a cab home.

Barbarella (Roger Vadim, 1968)

Roger Vadim used a French comic character as inspiration for this homage to his then wife's playful sexuality which, depending on your mood, you'll find either trite or wonderful. From Fonda's famous strip during the opening credits, you're in a forty-first-century fantasia: she slips seductively out of her clothes until she's naked, her intimate spots covered coyly by a forearm, or the lettering of the title sequence. The strip takes a fetishistic look at her figure-hugging jump-suit too, which would admittedly be more so if she were to slip *into* it.

Fonda plays the eponymous heroine, a special agent tasked with tracking down the sybaritic super-villain Duran Duran to the sensuously evil planet of SoGo. It's a lawful-order versus sensual chaos theme. Held captive by the Black Queen of SoGo, played wonderfully by Anita Pallenberg, Barbarella is subjected to all manner of indignities and forced pleasures which, in comic-book style, it's her patriotic duty to the planet Earth to grin and bear. Despite teaming up with a blind, Adonis-like angel, Barbarella is obliged to submit to kinky tortures: flesh-eating robot dolls rip her skimpy outfit to pieces while she's tied up; she's locked in a bird cage while a horde of angry birds shred another. On account of her ready smile and unfeasible pain threshold, these trials pass both for the kittenish Barbarella and for the viewer in a codeine-like fluffy haze, as Barbarella wins out through her capacity to find sheer pleasure in every extremity.

Finally, Barbarella must face Duran Duran himself and the mother of all camp tortures: the excessive machine. Luckily, she has had the foresight to strip off beforehand, and her sexual stamina once again stands her in good stead: Barbarella's a superhero, although her special power is not the ability to fly, or spin a web any size, but to be a complete slut – thus does she save planet Earth, and end up with the handsome angel too, who's a gender-inverted version of a Bond babe. The film also takes the use of devices and applies a Q-like ingenuity to weapons of forced sexual pleasure. Overarchingly camp but not in the least ironic, *Barbarella's* a fetishistic ode to Jane Fonda's body and the futuristic costumes that clad it, and you will either love or loathe its one-track-mindedness.

Barbarella and Duran Duran, though, both owe something to the heroes and villains of vaudeville and the silent era. Lara Croft and Trinity from the *Matrix* films, by contrast, are just as much fetish objects – with their figure-hugging, form-fitting fashions for post-feminist action women – but they're obliged to high-kick and kill as filmic shorthand for their independence and sexual liberation.

Belle de Jour (Luis Buñuel, 1967)
Séverine Serizy, played by the lustrous Catherine Deneuve, is a prosperous, bored housewife who takes to prostitution as her new leisure interest. This isn't, of course, a needle-friendly massage parlour of provincial England but the upscale house of a Parisian madam who asks no questions of so decorous and submissive an asset as Séverine.

While her unsuspecting husband, with whom she can't become aroused, is at work as a doctor in a hospital, Séverine also enjoys vividly perverse fantasies of domination, in which she is suspended from a tree and whipped by a dismissive, masterful aristocrat who then turns his back on her, considering her fit only for his servants. Throughout the film, Deneuve sports some fantastic designer couture suits by Yves St Laurent.

Belle de Jour is masterfully filmed by Spanish surrealist Buñuel, but somehow it doesn't touch the sides, and Deneuve doesn't ever seem fulfilled, perhaps because throwing off one's bourgeois manners so consciously is just so … bourgeois.

Blue Velvet (David Lynch, 1986)

It's difficult to do justice in a paragraph to a movie that whole books have been written about, but suffice to say that all the Ds apply: disturbing, deranged, dangerous, dark … especially dark. Beneath the white picket fences of Lumberton (small town America) lies a seething hell of twisted desires. Geoffrey Beaumont (Kyle MacLachlan) finds a severed ear on some scrubland near his home and, before he knows what he's into, he's witnessing – as a voyeur – the sexually depraved relationship between the terrifying nitrous oxide-sniffing maniac Frank (Dennis Hopper in his most relished role) and abused nightclub singer Dorothy Valance (Isabella Rossellini). When Frank takes 'neighbour' Geoffrey for a 'joyride', along with a wonderful menagerie of sleazy chums, Geoffrey's life is set to change for ever.

Like his cinematic surrealist antecedents, Buñuel and Dali, Lynch relishes teasing out the darkest parts of the unconscious and making them into art. His genius of vision has made this one of the most significant contributions to psychological cinema in history – as well as providing us with some beautifully ironic dialogue. A must-see movie of epic importance to those with an interest in sadism, masochism, surrealism, psycho-analysis and art.

Cat People (Jacques Tourneur, 1942)

The mysterious and beautiful Irena (Simone Simon) is a New York fashion artist – but don't let her smart little business suits fool you. She is in fact descended from an ancient group of Serbian women who were afflicted with the 'curse of the cat people' – meaning they morph into ravenous big cats when aroused. This is not ideal, as it means Irena cannot consummate her marriage to her beloved husband. He turns to a female colleague for 'consolation', but this 'normal' girl is then stalked by a shadowy presence lurking in the darkness, most wonderfully shot in an indoor swimming pool at night. Director Tourneur and producer Val Lewton are masters of horror by suggestion, and manage to evoke the terror of unseen things that emerges from the realm of the numinous – but without resorting to the obvious. Irena is sent to a shrink, and hubby thinks that they will soon be able to trace the source of her anxiety, but the psychiatrist can't figure it out – and he certainly cannot prevent her from hanging out at the local zoo and exchanging meaningful glances with the glossiest, darkest pumas. In fact, the shrink releases her inner beast, although we never see her transformation, and the film is all the more moody and powerful because of its understatedness. There is much here to delight the sophisticated fetishist with an eye for feline aesthetics and the latent wish that there can indeed be a covenant between women and cats. Forget the 1982 remake and delight in the subtlety of the original.

Crash (David Cronenberg, 1997)

The controversy that surrounded bringing J.G. Ballard's notorious piece of 70s nihilism to celluloid has been documented extensively elsewhere, but the furore created by its release detracted from one of the most magnificently arresting sequences of fetishistic emotion in cinema: that of Rosanna Arquette in leg calipers showing her appreciation for the sleek black vehicles in a car showroom. She caresses them in near-orgasmic frenzy, asking the bespectacled showroom manager if she can take one for a test drive, delighting in his squirming discomfort as part of her calipered leg snags the leather upholstery. For so many reasons this is forbidden imagery: her disability is presented as a fetish, and she plays up to it; James Spader (playing James Ballard) caresses the huge Cronenberg signature scar that runs up the back of her thigh; the close proximity of her tender twisted flesh against all that metal is a deliciously unwholesome juxtaposition. The camera invites you to imagine how it would feel to caress her as she caresses the cars. Underneath her tight black skirt, those fishnets and metal calipers would feel so much more pronounced than a flimsy suspender belt and stocking tops. You know that after one feel of that you would never go back to nylons.

Diary of a Chambermaid (Luis Buñuel, 1965)

A wonderfully pouty Jeanne Moreau stars as Celestine, a young chambermaid in perfect black starched dress, white pinny and frilled hat. Her boots, *les petites bottines*, are fawned over and confiscated by the elderly patriarch of the house, who spirits them to his own quarters for reasons one imagines are somewhat less than innocent. Buñuel said he thought it was his most erotic film, yet there is not a single sex scene. The fetish cognoscenti will certainly agree with him, knowing that the sight of the patriarch making Moreau walk up and down the room, trembling slightly on her high-heeled *bottines*, qualifies more admirably in the erotic history of cinema than any number of tumultuous sex scenes.

Les Diaboliques (Georges Henri Clouzot, 1962)

An unwholesome female stalks the corridors of a boys' boarding school in rural France with evil on her mind. No, not a prowler, but the headmaster's bit on the side. Simone Signoret cuts an uncompromising dash of frosty style as a whisky-drinking, Gitane-smoking, Ray-Ban-wearing bundle of blonde brittle loathing. Not since this masterpiece of mental cruelty and murderous intent has anyone worn a belted raincoat with such perverse aplomb. Duping feeble-bodied teacher and headmaster's wife Marianne Clouzot into committing what the poor creature thinks is a justifiable murder of her brutish husband, Signoret's character reeks of amorality. This power dynamic of the timid, vulnerable accomplice to the amoral, physically striking dominant is European narrative cinema's unholy female pairing par excellence. Drowning the brutish hubby, Signoret shows not a trace of apprehension or remorse when she places a marble weight on his chest to aid his watery demise. At a whim she strikes Marianne Clouzot sharply across the cheek to stop her pathetic snivelling, and you just know she would hog-tie you as soon as look at you.

It isn't love that binds Signoret to the headmaster, and one assumes their bond is one of sexual perversion, yet there isn't a single scene in the movie that spells this out literally. It's all between the lines, if you know where to look. Whilst there is little in the way of obvious fetishism or aberrant sexuality, the psychological cruelty that runs through the film is pure sadism.

Signoret herself is the ultimate phallic woman – hard, upright, always in heels and gloves, yet vulnerable to losing that power which, of course, in the denouement, she does – caught bang to rights by a private detective. Yet the thought of her in the women's prison opens up a whole new vista of fantasies.

Der Blaue Engel/The Blue Angel (Josef von Sternberg, 1930)

Immanuel Rath (Emil Jannings), an upstanding, stentorian schoolmaster in a small German town, finds that some of the boys in his class have been visiting a local *keller* in which cabaret singer Lola Lola performs. Intending to have a stiff word with her, he visits the club and is entranced by a cinematic vision that's as famous as Chaplin's and much nicer – Dietrich, skewed top hat and bare thighs, astride a chair, performing 'Falling in Love Again'.

Rath falls for Lola, squanders his savings and gives up his job. In thrall to her, the rest of his life degenerates. Consumed by his desire to worship at Lola's thighs, and tormented by his own rigidity, he marries and follows her until he is forced to return to his home town and appear as a clown there. After the performance has ended scandalously, Lola leaves him for another man. Deprived of his status and moral self-image, Rath becomes a truly poignant figure with no reason to live.

The Blue Angel's plot could be from Sacher-Masoch, a tale of a man brought low by the corrupting effects of a woman. But Rath's as much a victim of the high-minded rectitude that requires him to make an honest woman of Lola as he is of Lola, who exploits it. In his broad-chested propriety, Rath is like General 'Buck' Turgidson (get it?) in Kubrick's *Dr Strangelove*, and can't find a balance. He can't allow himself to be grateful for losing a few precious bodily fluids without giving up the things he's worked for, and doesn't know when to pay Lola off.

In Dietrich's Lola, meanwhile, we've an iconic image that's asserted its fashion subtly ever since. Most recently, Alison Goldfrapp borrowed her cocked top hat for her band's *Black Cherry* album. Dietrich herself became a US citizen in 1939 and, in an ironic twist of history, became a darling of US troops in World War II. She never made her peace with her native country, remarking in 1960, 'The Germans and I no longer speak the same language,' and lived in Paris until her death in 1992. But she's buried in Berlin and left her estate to the city in which she had been born in 1901. Bisexual, androgynous, Dietrich was the longest living connection to the fetishistic days of Weimar Berlin, where she had thrived as a woman in her twenties, and which informs the image of Lola from her top hat to her toenails.

Blue Hawaii (Norman Taurog, 1961)

Not a fetish film, of course: in fact, the finest of teen summer flicks and so good a vehicle for Elvis Presley's talents that he spent his film career trying to recreate it. The still young Elvis is a carefree beach bum living paradisiacally in Hawaii and wondering from time to time what to do with his life, besides wooing Jenny Maxwell, played by actress Jenny Lee. It's thought of as the King's capitulation, post-army, to becoming neutered and safe.

Nonetheless, it features a scene that would have made the cast of *Summer Holiday* blush.

Young Jenny Maxwell is suffering from self-pity and tries to drown herself in the sea. Hero Elvis is on hand and drags her out, bedraggled, her clothes clinging to her. She tells Elvis that nobody cares for or loves her, and that everybody hates her. Elvis tells her that nobody hates her and – in a revolutionary treatment for depression – that what she needs is a good old-fashioned spanking. Jenny replies that nobody has ever cared for her enough to do that. He then puts her across his knee and spanks her ass, which is covered by her dripping wet skirt.

To a modern viewer, the scene is jaw-droppingly, eye-poppingly comic, coming as it does after a suicide attempt, albeit an impetuous, petulant one, and you get the impression that, in a spirit of 'well, it's in the script', the actors went for it with alacrity. This is pre-feminist domestic violence, of the kind that has Jenny batting her eyelashes, looking skyward and thinking, He must really care, in Stepford-Wife fashion. Elvis plants fourteen firm spanks as Jenny yells loudly, before the scene changes to Jenny sitting on several cushions at the dinner table. Jenny Lee's face is a picture of outrage, so either she's a good actor or Elvis is getting into his role, which is a possibility: Priscilla Presley once admitted in an interview that the King sometimes liked her to dress up as a schoolgirl and spanked her when she was bad. Whether Priscilla herself enjoyed this or not, she didn't make clear, but we have a new Elvis to add to the pantheon of images his legend has created: the spanking Elvis. Blue Hawaii indeed.

Conspirators of Pleasure (Jan Svankmajer, 1996)

In this Czech film, six outwardly average individuals have elaborate fetishes they indulge with surreptitious care. A mousy letter carrier makes dough balls she grotesquely ingests before bed. A shop clerk fixates on a TV newsreader while he builds a machine to massage and masturbate himself. One of his customers makes an elaborate chicken costume for a voodoo-like scene with a doll resembling his plump neighbour. She, in turn, has a doll that resembles him, which she whips and dominates in an abandoned church. The TV newsreader has her own fantasy involving carp. Her husband, who is indifferent to her, steals materials to fashion elaborate artefacts of fur and pins that he rubs, scrapes and rolls across his body.

Six Degrees of Separation with strange suburban solo sex, the film is all the stranger because it unfolds without dialogue, like a Jacques Tati film but kinky and intimately perverse.

Equus (Sidney Lumet, 1977)

A film adaptation of the play by Peter Shaffer, *Equus* stars Richard Burton as Martin Dysart, a psychiatrist who takes on an unusual case: a young stable boy, played by the angelic Peter Firth, who prefers horses to Jenny Agutter, whose character also helps in the stables, and has blinded six of them in a frenzy. Their sessions reveal that the boy has a quasi-religious sexual fetish for the elemental power of the equine body, and he rides in the dead of night, experiencing an ecstasy unlike anything Dysart himself has ever known. Dysart begins to question whether the pursuit of normality is worth the loss of creative individual passions.

The therapy scenes are mildly absurd crescendos of revelation and insights, but drive the plot, as Dysart pulls the details of his threateningly religious home life from the boy, whose passionate midnight equestrianism has its own evocative vocabulary and ritual in the saddling up and use of tack. Inspired by contemporary views of the playwright's own homosexuality as a psychological disorder, *Equus* is a dated but powerful take on fetish as paraphilia. Burton, handsome and haggard, comes to realise that the boy's vision of the power of the horse may be lost to the world, and to loathe himself as the agent of a grey and passionless society. Also featuring Joan Plowright, it's top-notch British cinema from the days when it had the courage to explore, and Peter Firth captures the fetid anticipation of perverse pleasure – here it's horses but it could be Hoovers – perfectly.

The horses also star: Lumet's direction captures the animals' muscular power, feral mystery and perennial victimhood at the hands of humankind. They stamp and whinny, all flared nostrils and fearfulness, to rear out of our collective unconscious like perversions themselves.

Faster, Pussycat! Kill! Kill! (Russ Meyer, 1969)

> 'What ya got for sin, Varla?'
> 'That depends, Boom-boom, on what ya got in mind.'

Wrestling in the dust in hot pants, spitting lines that could psychologically damage for life and bearing sensational cleavages, Russ Meyer's comic-strip starlets inject extra sleaze into a desert adventure conceived on Bad Girl Boulevard. Cat-suited übervixen Tura Satana snaps the neck of an all-American jock after beating him into second place in a desert road race – just because she can. Whooee! This is the movie that saw the heavily breasted woman as a danger zone go into overdrive. Who ever said the female was castrated? These women have more balls than a Lotto rollover. Tura and her two stacked, wayward sidekicks play fast and loose with decency and the law in a rip-snorting rollicking theatre of cruelty that must have blown the brains out of any unsuspecting matinee punters who caught this little number back in the day with a box of popcorn: 'Hey honey, let's check this Pussycat thing out!'

Kidnapping the jock's saccharine cutey-pie fiancée, the testy trio find themselves at the ranch-cum-farmhouse of a wily old cripple and his hunky dumb son ('the vegetable') who it is rumoured have a load of cash stashed in the desert. With their cat's eyes on the loot, the girls' good manners go out of the window and murder, mayhem, whisky abuse and a whole heap of unwholesome behaviour ensues. The dialogue flies around like so many sharpened knives: when the old man says he couldn't have made a lecherous grab for the kidnapped young girl as he is stuck in his wheelchair, Varla tells him he should be nailed to it.

The film is a hoot from start to finish, the roles are relished by their perfectly cast actors and the underlying sleaze factor is a must for pervs with a retro eye. At the flimsiest excuse, the teenage cutie-pie is bitch-slapped and threatened with being tied up and gagged for whingeing (inappropriate when her boyfriend's freshly dead at the hands of Varla) and we get to see her actually tied to the steering wheel of Varla's car, ladies and gentlemen, in a polka-dot hair-bow and bikini. Hubba hubba. The framing of the choicest shots makes the most of the tight jeans and strong womanly forms of the three women – in contrast to the 'barely legal poppet in peril', who spends the entire film in a ripped shirt and bikini bottoms. Trucks, girl-on-girl action at the wheels of V8 roadsters, sick jokes and cutie-pie bondage. And Tura Satana. You need no further excuse. Watch with a bottle of bourbon and flick knife and go straight to hell without passing Go.

If ... (Lindsay Anderson, 1968)

If ... is a film that divides audiences. It was never a success in America, and is even less likely to be understood as allegorical there after the Columbine massacre. But it is an unflinching view of the dynamics of power and corporal punishment. If the past is another country, then the English public-school life of *If* is as far away from Hogwarts as you can get. Malcom McDowell was cast in *A Clockwork Orange* on account of his performance in this.

Handsome, floppy-haired and subject to the tight-trousered beatings and brutality of the school prefects, McDowell's schoolboy discovers his inner existentialist-anarchist and a world of motorbikes and biker-café girls, and wreaks a symbolic revenge on the school, despite the gradual concessions of its liberalising headmaster. As the anatomy of revolution, it's spot-on: it was the 1960s, man, and Brits like Lindsay Anderson didn't have a war to protest, so they picked on the vestiges of empire.

Despite switching confusingly between black and white and colour, it's also a fetishistic picture of the cloistered, disciplined, ritualised world in which desexualised CP thrived as the English Vice.

McLintock! (Andrew V. McLagen, 1963)
John Wayne's image continues to stand tall for many Americans. So representative was he of the square-jawed, World War II-era American male that Stalin and the KGB hatched a plot to assassinate him.

Wayne and Maureen O'Hara were born to star in *The Taming of the Shrew*, and this movie is the closest they got. Wayne plays a cattle baron whose estranged wife (O'Hara) wants a divorce. The film is one long comic brawl between them, culminating in a mud-pit melée after which Wayne drags O'Hara into a barn and spanks her roundly in front of an assembled throng, a man with a redder shade of neck giving a woman a redder shade of bottom. This might raise a chuckle or, if you find John Wayne objectionable, prove more disturbing than *Necro Hell II: The Bitch-Brides of Satan*. Rough 'n' ready Wayne has a reputation as a cinematic spanker, but other than *McLintock!* only really delivered one in *Donovan's Reef* (filmed the same year – wonder if his hand was sore). That *palm d'or* goes to Tim Holt, a B-movie Western actor who dished out a spanking to his leading ladies in no less than three B-movies.

Maîtresse (Barbet Schroeder, 1976)
A young Gérard Depardieu (27 at the time) features in *Maîtresse*, and that's probably the reason you're likely to see this notoriously scandalous film, which tells the story of a thief named Olivier who

robs the apartment of a mild-mannered woman (Bulle Ogier) he's encountered earlier in the day. Much to his surprise, he discovers a dungeon on her bottom floor. Ogier's Ariane is secretly a dominatrix, stomping on genitals, stretching clients on a rack, encaging, entombing and otherwise abusing her johns to a pitch of ecstatic release. This discovery leads to all manner of unexpected high jinks, as Olivier and Ariane begin a torrid affair while he watches her at work. Olivier becomes obsessed with one of Ariane's clients, a horse is slaughtered on camera and a horsemeat *filet* is consumed in the following scene.

Don't be fooled, though; the film wears its fetishism on its leather sleeve, to hook a flared and uninitiated 1970s audience with its freak-show value. The dungeon scenes aren't bad – the subs weren't professional actors but fetish-scene slaves – but otherwise the film is full of strokes that are broader than those from Ariane's whip. At work Ariane wears a black Louise Brooks wig, but with Depardieu she shakes down her blonde tresses as if the wig's required by the French equivalent of the Health and Safety at Work Act. This is in case you didn't get the idea that the dominant whore is able to be a submissive Madonna in his company, in which state of mind, of course, she finds her true liberation. You suspect this is Schroeder's personal vision of any healthy Frenchwoman. This is wish-fulfilment for straight people who fancy a perv.

We're supposed to think of the fetish elements as alluding to the ugliness behind the otherwise beautiful walls of Paris, but Paris, unintentionally, looks a whole lot uglier on the outside. You wonder about this mismatched relationship between a dangerous housebreaker and the woman who surrenders her independence to him. Perhaps because Depardieu's Depardieu, Ariane seems deluded by her love, and you're asked to believe that Olivier's real world of crime is somehow superior to a bit of victimless paid SM. In affecting a world-weary insouciance, the film collapses every moral distinction – of course perverts are going to hobnob naturally with housebreaking stalkers. Instead of simpering, you wish Ogier would fetch Depardieu the ball-stomping stiletto he deserves, and drop him off with the *gendarmerie* in a pair of her frilly panties. In the end it's annoying tosh, best enjoyed, if you must, by turning off your brain and ogling Ogier.

The Matrix (Andy & Larry Wachowski,1999)

'You're here because you know something,' says Larry Fishburne's Morpheus to Keanu Reeves' Neo in *The Matrix*. 'What you know you can't explain – but you feel it. You've felt it your entire life; that there's something wrong with the world; you don't know what it is, but it's there, like a splinter in your mind, driving you mad. It is this feeling that has brought you to me.

'You can feel it when you go to work, when you go to church, when you pay your taxes; it is the world that has been pulled over your eyes to blind you from the truth.'

Neo asks, 'What truth?'

'That you are a slave, Neo, like everyone else, you were born into bondage; born into a prison that you cannot smell or taste or touch; a prison for your mind.'

Young Neo, so it seems, is a computer hacker who lives in a future-world not unlike our own, until he is contacted by a subversive and sinister organisation which is determined to introduce him, for reasons that are messianic and allegorical, to the true nature of reality. Morpheus invites him to partake of the tree of knowledge, in the form of a pill, and tear the veil from his own eyes. Or else he can choose another pill and return to his life with no knowledge of their meeting, ignorant of the truth. When the real nature of his existence is revealed to him, he spends the rest of the first film on a quest to find out if he may be the one who can change these dystopic circumstances for all humankind, high-kicking his way in militaristic leather and dark-glasses, in a plot twist that is actually the *antidote* to conventional Hollywood violence.

Any self-respecting silicone messiah would benefit from the back-up of a strong woman like Trinity (Carrie-Anne Moss), who wields phallic weaponry while clad head-to-toe in shimmering rubber often enough to keep the isotonic-drink and talcum-powder industries going single-handed. *The Matrix*, and the far less decipherable *Matrix Reloaded*, are masterworks of futuresex imagery, from the heroes' clothes to the bizarre, insect-like, *Alien*-influenced world through which the *Nebuchadnezzar* spaceship travels; the pods in the power plants, their human contents in symbiotic full-enclosure bondage with their mechanical overlords; and the bleak world of Machine City. The film becomes a biomechanical masterpiece of machines made flesh. Well, which pill would you take?

Merry Christmas, Mr Lawrence (Nagisa Oshima, 1983)

Set in a Japanese POW camp in Java in 1942, *Merry Christmas, Mr Lawrence* is based on a Laurens van der Post story, *The Seed and the Sower*. It's an involving and incredibly humane film. While David Bowie and Ryuichi Sakamoto's names are at the top, the linchpin of the film is Tom Conti as the eponymous British officer, a translator trying to reconcile his respect for Japanese culture with the barbarity of the POW camp. Aside from a curious flashback sequence in which he impersonates a schoolboy, Bowie is actually darn good as Major Jack 'Strafer' Celliers, a mysterious and spirited 'man's man' who has a beguiling effect on the young officer commanding the camp, Captain Yonoi (Sakamoto), an anglophile who quotes Shakespeare as he issues brutal orders, expressing his love by using his power until Celliers is inhumed, his bloated head reminiscent of a scene in Mirbeau's *The Torture Garden*.

As Lawrence says to a Japanese officer facing execution after the war, he is now the victim of men who are sure they are right, just as in the camp the Japanese were sure they were right. The film has a political message but that isn't the reason it's in this book: *Senjou no Merii Kurisumasu* is probably the only film to feature two giants of electronica, and Sakamoto scored the film, including the theme 'Forbidden Colours'. The music conjures up the atmosphere of regret, lost love and repressed heartbreak that we see in the unrequited feelings Sakamoto's character has for Bowie's. Yonoi's human instincts have no place in the wartime world he inhabits, and he can only express them by Sadeian means. In some ways we are constrained by such roles as if it's always wartime, and *Merry Christmas, Mr Lawrence* dissects the anatomy of this desire.

The Night Porter (Liliana Cavani, 1974)

Dirk wore white socks, as Adam Ant noted in 1978, but he also wore a very fetching uniform in Liliana Cavani's overrated 1974 picture, where the thoughtful manners of the cinema of alienation bump awkwardly into the 1970s taste for Nazi-sploitation, and two fine actors, Charlotte Rampling and Dirk Bogarde, turn in sensitive performances in an inherently unbelievable situation. Bogarde is a former concentration camp guard who now slinks surreptitiously around the hotel where he works as a night porter, part of a covert group of ex-Nazis devoted to hiding their past. Rampling is a guest, once a camp inmate, now prosperous, and the two rekindle a needy SM passion which is semi-explicit, soft-focus and darned impossible, if classily filmed. Rampling's character is a Jew, so apart from being unbelievable the film suggests that perverts have no self-respect.

Bogarde's naughty Nazi is a furrow-browed picture of dominant angst, while it's to Rampling's credit if she makes you believe she's happy to see him again. The couple pay the price for their obsession with each other, and that hoary, moralistic old connection between obsessional love and death – which is only as real as you want to make it – is made again.

The Night Porter was inspired by both the mainstream success of *Last Tango in Paris*, made two years earlier, and the US popularity of Nazi-sploitation schlockers, which peaked with Tinto Brass's *Salon Kitty* (probably the most watchable of its kind, in being brothel- rather than camp-based) and *Ilsa: She-Wolf of the SS*. There was a legion of Italian *il sadiconazista* movies that pushed the envelope of taste past splitting-point. Ironically, the Nazi-sploitation genre was a by-product of the censorship of its day. Sex and swastikas sold in the 1970s, and film-makers had discovered that it was easier to get sex 'n' violence past the censors if they were presented as having a historical basis in Nazi atrocities, even though the films themselves weren't interested in historical accuracy.

Although the film is pretty dire in terms of dialogue, it brought about one of European cinema's most controversial and striking movie posters of all time: la Rampling bare-chested, ribs proud, in braces and a Nazi officer's hat.

Nine ½ Weeks (Adrian Lyne, 1996)

In the most memorable scene in this film, Kim Basinger crawls reluctantly across the floor, picking up bills dropped by Mickey Rourke. It's powerful because it's uncomfortably close to why she'd be in this film at all. She works demurely in an art gallery, O'Rourke does something mysterious in Wall Street. Together they embark on a 1980s West Coast idea of an edgy East Coast relationship. When O'Rourke does menacing, he's just ratty, Kim Basinger is only called on to be beautiful, even though she can act, and New York is a cartoon city straight out of casting. This is soft-focus Kimsploitation: treacle on the thighs? Chillies in your mouth? Things that look great to the camera wouldn't feel as great as they're faking, but neither does the script allow for giggling. An implausible film that takes itself too seriously by half.

Pirates of the Caribbean: Curse of the Black Pearl (Gore Verbinsky, 2003)

Johnny Depp has spent his cinema career with only one foot in reality, the other in imagination. Many of his film roles have been semi-fetishistic, fairy-tale sinister transformations: from the body-suited, half-finished form of Edward Scissorhands, whose disability is its own form of bondage, to pirate captain Jack Sparrow, who prances and minces with kohl-eyed camp as he buckles his swash. Depp was inspired by Keith Richards, but his performance also reflects how camp the traditional image of the buccaneering pirate of old Hollywood films now seems anyway.

The myths of piracy have provided a lexicon of fetishistic imagery that inspired Vivienne Westwood's 'pirate look' in the early 1980s. Feathered tricorn hats, parrots and pieces-of-eight are nothing like the realities of hard-pressed lives and naval cast-offs, of course, and even the much-romanticised women pirates such as Anne Bonney were in reality pretty rum characters, but the appeal of their anarchic freedoms has a life of its own. Eye-patches, peg-legs, doubloons and treasure chests refer to it, while hanging from the yard-arm or walking the plank is all good pirate fun.

Jack Sparrow is short on plunder and long on words, but even so Depp's every move is informed by pirate myth, while Keira Knightley is an ironic damsel in distress with lusts of her own. The first *Pirates of the Caribbean* film is politically correct Disney throughout, based as it is on a theme-park ride. But, even if you think of Disney as a mind-controlling mega-corporation, you're going to have to flirt with Uncle Walt at some point if you want to get hip to modern fairytales.

La Prisonnière (Georges Henri Clouzot, 1968)

Secretary (see p. 139) doesn't come close to this emotionally brutal but visually stunning treatment of sub/dom relationships, although it is almost impossible to view as the film has never been transferred to home cinema format. An obsessive, dominant Op Art gallery owner, played by the handsome Laurent Terzieff, is an enthusiastic amateur photographer to whom mentally fragile but addictively interesting women are attracted. They secretly volunteer to pose near-naked in crinkly plastic coats and be scrutinised by his lens. Their motivation is low self-esteem; his is something similar but altogether more calculated, though no less damaged. Meanwhile, the straight, bright young things choose to network in the gallery, dreaming of bourgeois achievements and unaware their boss/mentor is a pervert. Occasionally Terzieff uses props or ties his models up. Sometimes he does two at a time, the girls taking a rest between set-ups, lounging, smoking and cracking and squeaking in their plastic. Before they subject themselves to his scrutiny he gives them a slide show of Man Ray-like images to prove he's not alone in his tastes.

The girlfriend of a local artist discovers his twilight world and becomes wildly aroused. She cannot stay away from him and he puts her through excruciating embarrassment in his office, making her say what it is she really wants from him, making her crawl about on all fours and be dominated by him. The SM dynamic is perfectly realised from this director, in his last film but also at the pinnacle of his nihilistic vision, unclouded by emotions other than brutality, bitterness and the desire to realise an aesthetic vision of beautiful cruelty unparalleled in narrative cinema – apart from *Les Diaboliques*, of course.

Scorpio Rising (Kenneth Anger, 1965)

If ever a film was about the fetishisation of *stuff*, then surely it is Anger's revolutionary, dark and provocative short. A homoerotic orgy of bad-boy behaviour, it begins sedately as we watch a couple of young bucks in their garage, polishing and greasing their enormous motorbikes to a cheesy backing track of teen hits of the time. The tempo picks up as we are treated to the delicious ritual of various slinky and sinewy studs getting dressed. Oh, the joy of the voyeuristic gay gaze as it realises that putting clothes on is so much more potent and full of promise than getting them off. Leather jackets slide on cold over naked shoulders; key chains are wound through jean belt loops and buckles are tightened. (Kathryn Bigelow must have been influenced by this sequence when she opened *Blue Steel* with Jamie Lee Curtis getting dressed for work in her cop uniform.)

We leave the garage and are in Scorpio's room. It's a treasure trove of boys' bits. We get skull rings, coasters, overflowing ashtrays, packets of Lucky Strike, Zippo lighters, scorpions-in-resin paper-weights, guns, torches, boots, James Dean memorabilia, knives and discarded newspapers. Teenage motorcycle cults are made of such things. Scorpio lights a match on his teeth and takes target practice at religious icons; he lounges, bored, stroking a Siamese cat. And there's Nazi regalia too, indulged in with satanic delight. Flash frames of Hitler are cut into scenes of the boys crashing a Halloween party. The backing track plays 'He'll always be my true love, my true love'. All you need to have a good time is a cop's flashlight and a gun.

The frenetic pace of the editing, which includes a montage of stock footage, dirt-bike trails and Bible stories, and the ironic rhythm of a backing track that wouldn't have sounded out of place in a Doris Day movie yet seem so very, very perverse here, were a first. As must have been the sight of a bloodied, whipped arse with a Nazi flag hanging in the background of the 'party' scene. Anger's vision has been unique in cinema. It's pared-down and beautiful and still sends an electrical charge of pure gleeful badness through the veins. Heil Satan!

Secretary (Steven Shainberg 2002)
Directed by Steven Shainberg, who made the ridiculous *Hit Me* (1996), and based on a short story by Mary Gaitskill, author of *Two*

Girls, Fat and Thin, *Secretary* looks like a turkey but turns out to be an endearing if formulaic romantic comedy, except with spanking instead of snogging – *When Harry Spanked Sally*. But the characters in *Secretary* wouldn't be so confident as to fake an orgasm in a diner. Maggie Gyllenhaal's titular secretary emerges blinking and fragile from a mental hospital and learns self-respect at the hands of boss James Spader's corrective therapy. Gyllenhaal is brave and gorgeous and Spader excellently shifty. The actors make the most of the fetid spanking, caning and masturbation scenes. Plausible and well worth watching for the first two-thirds before it strains towards a studio ending. The bottom on the poster? That's not Gyllenhaal's.

The Servant (Joseph Losey, 1963)
A taut screenplay by Harold Pinter based on a Robin Maugham novel, directed by the underrated and ahead-of-his-time Losey, *The Servant* stars Dirk Bogarde as steely butler Hugo Barrett and James Fox as his feckless employer, Tony. The pair are a dark version of Wodehouse's Jeeves and Wooster, as Barrett spins a web of psychological domination, typical of Pinter's work such as *The Caretaker*, around the nice-but-dim aristocrat and his snotty girlfriend Wendy Craig. Oxbridge twit Tony is dramatically enslaved by his contemptuous butler in a homoerotic, pervy take on class war.

Sex and Zen (Michael Mak, 1993)
Staring the lustrous Amy Yip, *Sex and Zen* will be known to many fans of Hong Kong cinema as a commendably bizarre, pornographic sex comedy. The film features the wince-inducing grafting of an equestrian penis on to its hero, played by Kent Cheng, as well as automated whipping machines, bizarre lesbian trysts and solo sex with a flute. Its denouement is the karmic payback in which the 'Before Midnight Scholar' is compelled to make love with the mare who has been deprived of sex thanks to the aforementioned surgery. Amazingly, although produced with cinematic aplomb, the

film is not that far removed from the book on which it's based, Li Yu's erotic classic *The Carnal Prayer Mat*, first published in China in 1634.

The hero is nicknamed the 'Before Midnight Scholar' on account of his unstoppable sex-drive, as he works his way through the women of his town. After he solves the problem of his under-endowment by the bizarre means above, there's no stopping him. Escaping from a jealous and vengeful husband, he finds himself imprisoned in a trunk belonging to a particularly powerful matron, where his sweat-sheened privations really begin, before he escapes to find his deserted wife now working in a brothel. In the end, his desires spent, he makes his peace with the world, but not without a fight. A mind-bending blend of *Carry On* humour and surreal pornography, *Sex and Zen* is a strange and beguiling film – an explicit morality tale.

¡Átame!/Tie Me Up, Tie Me Down (Pedro Almodovar, 1990)

Victoria Abril and the unlikely Antonio Banderas star in this strange beast from the acclaimed Spanish director. Ricky is released from a mental hospital and kidnaps Marina, a former porn star with whom he once had sex, hoping to make her love him through sheer application of the Stockholm Effect. It's a straightforward filmic approach to a subject usually dealt with more fantastically.

Les Yeux Sans Visage (Georges Franju, 1959)

In Franju's dark fairytale portrait of beauty and terror, anxiety is never far away. Domineering surgeon Pierre Brasseur has left his beloved daughter grotesquely facially disfigured as a result of his crashing their car by reckless driving. She spends her days shut away in the family mansion, wearing an expressionless plaster mask, wanly combing her hair and hoping in vain that daddy will be able to perfect a face transplant and make her beautiful again. Shiny-black-plastic-mac-wearing nurse/helper Alida Valli is regularly dispatched in her 2CV (complete with incongruous use of background carnival music) to hunt down young pretty women whose faces will be cut off in the hope that one may be a suitable donor. There is much sweating in medical apparel and the application of sharp instruments as Brasseur and Valli attempt to perform the transplant. Needless to say, the project is futile – and it is Valli who bears the brunt of its failure and Brasseur's impotence at effecting a cure. Although the daughter gets to experience a few days with a 'normal' new face, it soon rots away, along with all hope.

Throughout this amazing film, which critics of the time slandered as being 'for perverts', there is much eeriness in the characters' necessity to break away from where or what they really are. From Edith Scob's fragile, childlike exploration of the attic in which she is confined for most of her day, to the startling image of an unfortunate captive's break for freedom in a tight sweater and fully bandaged head (an uncanny disquieting sight), despair and madness seep into every frame. Dominant males play God with fragile, 'flawed' females at all turns: apart from the surgeon/fanatic, there are the cops investigating numerous girls' disappearances who think nothing of using a cute young shoplifter as a decoy, knowing she will undergo medical experiments. 'No, please, not the encephalograph!' Nature has her way at the film's end as Scob releases the vivisection dogs to savage their captor – her hated father – and, as the mask is left behind, she wanders free into the night with the dogs and her pet doves following.

Three Movies with Pervery as a Central Theme

Fetishes (Nick Broomfield, 1996)

After *Touching the Void* and *Bowling for Columbine*, documentary is more and more considered part of mainstream cinema. For two weeks in 1996, Nick Broomfield and a documentary crew visited Pandora's Box, an upscale house of bondage on Manhattan's Fifth Avenue, where clients pay $175 an hour to be subservient to mistresses. For the heavyweight Broomfield, more used to subjects such as Biggie and Tupac, Margaret Thatcher, Kurt and Courtney, sinned-against serial killer Aileen Wuornos, and, when it comes to paid sex, the trial of Heidi Fleiss, filming *Fetishes* must have been a relaxing break; anything that's technically illegal here is certainly a victimless crime. Mistresses talk about their craft; a few clients, usually masked, are interviewed as well. Then, the camera watches sessions organised around fetishes: wrestling, lots of rubber, corporal punishment, masochism and adult babies. Mistress Raven, the owner of Pandora's Box, gives us the pep-talk that pain may or may not be part of the subservient experience; it is, at its root, a transfer of power. After their session has ended, clients talk about how drained, relaxed, relieved and at peace they are. We're so used to the cheap programming of late-night cable-style reality sex shows that, on seeing subjects chatting surrounded by the paraphernalia of SM, it takes a moment to realise you are watching a thoughtful and positive film.

Personal Services (Terry Jones, 1987)

Not a fetish film, but a sweet bio-pic comedy with cuffs and rubber. Sure-footedly acted, not at all explicit, this film is inspired by the rise and fall of Cynthia Payne, one of the best-known madams in Britain's history. Julie Walters plays Christina, a woman who evolves from a waitress struggling to cover her rent to a successful businesswoman running a brothel that caters to the discriminatingly kinky. This being David Yelland's suburban London, it has something of the realism of *Room at the Top*. Baroque fantasy it isn't. The clients are all fine, upstanding Englishmen in search of submissive pleasure, and solicit it as if they have a gardening query. As well as running her house, Christina raises a son, forces her father to come to terms with the person his daughter has become and, not surprisingly with hindsight, despairs of ever finding the 'Charles and Diana' ideal of love for herself.

In one scene, a tart pathetically tries to escape a copper who's tackling her, angel's wings flapping in a moonlit garden like her useless aspirations. The circumstances of a missed straight date hint at the old chestnut that whores are doomed to die lonely. Nevertheless, the johns' passionless reserve, the tarts' insights into their sexuality, and the *Carry On* meets *Keeping up Appearances* quality make *Personal Services* a picture of a world of Miss Whiplash and lace doilies that's as bygone as Joyce Grenfell's. The tarts are working-class versions of the same redoubtable Englishness as hers. It's a portrait of straight-faced English silliness, with a frankly unerotic sense of the ordinariness of it all.

Preaching to the Perverted (Stuart Urban, 1997)
Starring luscious lesbian Guinevere Turner as dominatrix Tanya Cheex, and featuring British cinema stalwarts such as Tom Bell, *Preaching to the Perverted* is brave and amusing. It has a visual lushness too.

Peter is the young acolyte of a moralistic government minister who thinks that nailing some SMers, as it were, will be a vote-winner. He is dispatched to check out the scene in order to build a case, and falls for the dom.

You'll want to like it, although it tries to walk an uneasy line, both making a case for fetishistic sex and making you laugh with good old British satire. Pitching a political satire with an SM theme – which after all, this side of blood-letting, edge-play or heavy CP, is a head-game that can be portrayed in some certificate-friendly, non-explicit ways – is going to interest the venture capitalists. The trouble is – if you'll forgive the cliché – it does exactly what it says on the tin. Anyone watching this film will be fetish-friendly and will get mileage from the comedy of manners, but a bit less earnestness might've made it more effective.

SEXPLOITATION HELL!

This is a book on fetish that's made it into the cultural mainstream, so you won't find a directory here of up-to-date porn films featuring spanking, SM and bondage. Porn titles even from quality filmmakers don't tend to stay on the shelves for long, whereas the films detailed above will be around, in one DVD edition or another, for some time to come. Nonetheless, there's a rich seam of cheesy, tacky, poor-taste fetish films which are available from mail-order suppliers.

These films make free with consent, safety and, for that matter, sanity, but then they weren't meant to be the *Kama Sutra*. Incredible though it is to think of today, in America these films were playing routinely at drive-ins well into the 1970s. Many of them follow, however loosely, a thriller plot, just as Nazi-sploitation films, which for all their offensiveness also played widely in drive-ins, were able to hang themselves on the peg of being historical. Whereas today it's not uncommon to find many self-identified porn films that parody mainstream releases, such as *Shaving Ryan's Privates*, in the 1960s and 1970s that opportunity didn't exist. Instead, the aim of these films was to provide a narrative opportunity to flash a whip or a pair of breasts across the screen, and to signpost to the viewer that they could expect a bit of that in the movie, while hanging on to a legitimising genre as much as was necessary to get distribution.

In the end, video killed the sexploitation star, just as the drive-ins are now superstores, when porn tapes were able to achieve professional distribution. Alongside porn videos, the now-tame 'video nasties' such as *Faces of Death* picked up the sophomoric schlock market. Not that sexploitation movies are missed – to watch sexploitation films is generally to watch a collection of motleys who were only there for the money, and this awareness makes the experience pretty tacky. So are porn actors, but there's no pretence that you're watching them for anything other than arousal, so the exchange seems fairer. In any case, here's a tacky top ten from a hidden history that cinema would rather forget:

10. The Pick Up (1968)
This rare David Friedman–Bob Cresse production is as sleazy as the day it was released. Set in Las Vegas, the film tells of two couriers who track down the two girls who stole cash they're carrying for the mob. Once caught, the gals are subjected to all sorts of depraved unpleasantness. Bob Cresse also produced the unmissably kitschy *Mondo* series of exploitation films.

9. Heat of Midnight (1966)
Sex-packed 'thriller' directed by Bob Cresse – again – about a man who steals jewels from a Parisian crime syndicate, then seeks shelter with his ex-wife, who now has a lesbian lover. Eventually, a group of mobsters abducts and tortures the lover in the hope of finding the location of the jewels. When a private detective intervenes, everyone has sex.

8. The Forbidden (1966)
A seedy study of the sordid customs of the world, or at least what passed for the world back when Asian sex tourism was something only US Navy sailors went for. See women learning karate in order to subdue would-be rapists; topless bars that float in swimming pools; Swedish lesbian clubs; and every vice to arouse a sleazy Phileas Fogg.

7. Hollwood's World of Flesh (1963)
A seedy look at what goes on behind the scenes in Tinseltown: casting couches, nude models, sex clubs, poolside orgies, Japanese bathhouses and more.

6. Some Girls Do (1967)
Not a 1970s hit from Sailor, but a kinky lesbian exploitation flick.

A farm girl arrives in New York City looking for sexual adventures and finds them when she rooms with two women who are into everything: lesbianism, prostitution, SM and other forms of kinkiness. When the country girl learns how mean men can be, she wreaks revenge.

5. Babette (1968)
A nasty little sex kitten involved in New York's underground sex scene joins forces with another sex-hungry babe, makes porn movies, lures a housewife into a threesome, takes part in a rubber-themed orgy and gets involved in the SM scene. A wild example of Big Apple sexploitation.

4. I Am for Sale (1968)
A group of former prostitutes purportedly recalls the perversions of its working experiences: a former stripper services a Latin lover who turns out to be a masochistic lesbian; a woman submits to a body painting session, then enjoys a threesome; and, for full sexploitation value, a madam gets surprised by a rough customer.

3. Massacre of Pleasure (1966)
Seamy sexploitation from Bob Cresse again, in which women are captured by a Parisian crime operation and given a choice: submit to their captors' sadistic demands or die. But some of the captive women begin to enjoy their SM lifestyle, which causes problems for the gang. This was, apparently, 'A shattering step forward in the sensual revolution of motion picture-making.'

2. The Sexploiters (1965)
An ultra-kinky shockathon from Bob Cresse. A suburban housewife seeking thrills in New York City joins a prostitution ring that's fronted by a model agency. Along with her coworkers, the woman teases her clients to ecstasy, but learns to appreciate the pleasures of other women too.

1. The Girls on F Street (1966)

Also known as *The Maidens of Fetish Street*, this is a more worth-while offering, and No.1 chiefly because it's extremely bizarre, with a whacked-out directorial style. A depressed old man – bear with it – recalls his friend's kinky sexual excursions in LA of the 1920s, then sets out to pleasure himself in unusual ways by checking out 'The House of Fetish'. On account of the budget for period detail, you can't tell whether you're in the 1920s or 1960s, which is half the appeal. There are whippings, two girls in a bath, a hilarious old sadist named Hilda and lots more kinky fun.

British Kinky Capers

While Americans were making non-consensual sexploitation shockers and the Italians were filming Nazi-sploitation, the British had the cosy, infuriating *Confessions Of …* flicks. Apart from the *Carry On* series, which was alive with fetishised doctors, nurses, matrons and toilet humour, the early 1970s saw the Brits wading into X-rated entertainment, seemingly unable to shake off the saucy vaudevillian style of Benny Hill.

The Ups and Downs of a Handyman (John Sealey, 1975)

British sex comedies are pretty much 'seen one, seen them all', but this one throws in so many clichés of the genre that it can represent the rest. It even includes that irritating old chestnut, speeded-up filming of sex chases. Yet it's hard to completely dislike a film that portrays everyone in Surrey as a raving pervert. And no film that subjects the viewer to the sight of spank-happy local squire Bob Todd naked in the shower but for a bowler hat, hand-spanking a beauty about twenty years his junior, can be accused of good taste.

On the other hand, we have …

House of Whipcord (Pete Walker, 1975)

Having learned the trade as a skin-flick man directing swinging titles like *Cool it, Carol* and *School for Sin*, Walker went on to make horror movies. Scripted by the prolific David McGillivray, *House of Whipcord* is set in a private house of correction, somewhere in the woodlands of Southern England, where a couple of bonkers disciplinarians are determined to teach young women with loose morals the errors of their ways – with the utmost severity. The overall atmosphere tends towards being as grim as it gets – imagine *Within These Walls* crossed with *Ghosts of the Civil Dead* – but from knowing Walker's other work, such as the wonderfully lurid *Frightmare*, we can assume that tongues were firmly in cheeks. Even so, it's to Walker's credit as a director that he was so easily able to switch his focus from comic horror to Sadeian spectacle. Definitely one for a rainy afternoon as an antidote to RomCom.

The Schlockmeisters: John Waters and Divine

Fascinated by extremes of behaviour and surreal sexual ridiculousness, schlockmeister John Waters grew up in suburban Baltimore, a teenage geek who began to make home movies that used his weird friends as actors. From his earliest work as a Warhol of small-town weirdness to the polished edgy-but-mainstream appeal of his current work, Waters' films betray the director's affection for his characters, however sick and depraved, while his mainstream stuff is positively life-affirming.

Pink Flamingos

Made in 1972, *Pink Flamingos* remains, despite his later more commercial productions, perhaps Waters' most representative and, well, seminal film. For all his acceptability since *Hairspray* (starring Ricki Lake!) he'd probably like it that way. Sleaze queen Divine lives in a trailer with her mad hippie son Crackers and her twenty-stone mother Mama Edie, trying to rest on their laurels as 'the filthiest people alive'. But competition arrives in the form of Connie and Raymond Marble, who deal heroin to schoolchildren and kidnap and impregnate female hitchers, so that they can sell the babies to lesbian couples. Finally, they challenge Divine directly, and the gross-out commences.

Made at the commercial height of the exploitation genre, *Pink Flamingos* is a trashy, deceptively throwaway homage from a fan with a camera. It could be lazily referred to as offensive, but it's anything but. Gross and virtually unwatchable parts of it may be, but it's so much more satirical and knowing in spirit than any of its influences. You know you're in safe hands, even though you won't look at poodles in the same way again.

The film owes much to the glorious Divine Trash (her surname was dropped later in her career), so larger than life that she blocks out the sun. Most remembered by some, perhaps, for the stomping hit 'You Think You're a Man', she was a TV terror who makes Lily Savage look like Lady Bracknell. Divine was free to cause chaos while Glen Milstead, her bald, fat, unremarkable creator from Baltimore, could stand back and smirk. Sadly, he died from a bad heart in 1998. Divine's version of transvestism was half-attractive and half-comedic, somewhere between a voguish, curvaceous TV with beautiful nails and Bernard Bresslaw in a bra. A strapped and stayed sex bomb with the manners of a builder, Divine was a man who became a woman who acted like a man – that's more method than Brando. Don't just take him for a bloke in a dress.

Mondo Trasho (1969), meanwhile, features a day in the lives of a hit-and-run driver and her victim, and the bizarre things that happen to them before and after their fates are intertwined: these everyday occurrences include ecstatic visions of the Virgin Mary, assault by a crazed foot-fetishist, and chicken-foot grafting operations. *Female Trouble* (1976) chronicles the life of Dawn Davenport, as we chart her progress from loving schoolgirl to crazed mass murderer – all on account of her parents' refusal to buy her cha-cha heels for Christmas. She runs away from home, is raped and becomes a single mother, criminal and glamorous model before her inevitable rendezvous with the chair.

Polyester (1981)
Divine comes of age, however, in *Polyester* (1981), a frankly surprising *tour de force* in which she plays a middle-aged, married, self-confessed good Christian woman coming apart at the seams. It has all of Waters' hilarious, camp hideousness, but is also an amusing middle-class satire. Unfortunately for the appearance-conscious Francine Fishpaw, the money to support her suburban lifestyle comes from her husband's porn cinema. The neighbours are protesting, her son turns out to be notorious foot-fetishist 'The Baltimore Stomper', her daughter is knocked up by a local crook and wants to be a stripper, and her husband is having an affair with his sleazy secretary. Despite the lovely gimmick of Odorama, in which early audiences were given scratch 'n' sniff cards to enhance their viewing pleasure, this is – whisper it quietly – a serious film.

FETISH ICON: EDWARD D. WOOD JR. (1924–1978)

Angora Management
(fetishes: x-dressing)

Most famous today on account of Tim Burton's 1994 biopic starring Johnny Depp, Ed Wood is remembered for the string of B-movies he made in Hollywood during the 1950s, which were so bad that critics re-classified them as 'Z-movies'. The best known is *Plan 9 from Outer Space*. The title has nothing to do with the movie whatsoever, and this is just the first of the strange examples of non-sequitousness in the film. You can't even describe the film as having continuity errors, because there are more errors than there is continuity. As late-night, camp, kitsch viewing, they're unsurpassed accidental masterpieces. Be terrorised by a man in a gorilla suit with a space helmet on his head!

If questions of aesthetics and taste are reduced to a utilitarian numbers game, then Ed Wood's films have given as many people as much pleasure as any coherent *meisterwerk* from an acclaimed surrealist director. In fact, Wood *is* a surrealist director; he just didn't know it.

Wood powered himself through the adversities of his career – not that there was much career between his adversities – with an unflappably quixotic belief that he could make decent films. Unfortunately, he died a forgotten, impoverished alcoholic at 54. Since then, audiences have moved from laughing at to laughing with him, and have made his self-confidence a self-fulfilling prophecy. It's a redemptive story, even though Wood himself didn't get to share in it, perhaps because it so perfectly taps into the self-invention of the American Dream.

It's typical, then, that his first feature-length production should have been about a subject as unexpected as the film is bad. Wood didn't do things by halves and so, having the chance to make a movie, he made one about the subject dearest to his heart: cross-dressing. *Glen or Glenda* (1952) is a shameless exploitation pic that also tries confusingly to be transgender PR. With its tag-line 'He loved women so much, he dressed like one', it's the tale of Glen or Glenda, told retrospectively from the point of view of a policeman investigating his suicide, who visits a psychologist – a x-dresser himself – and gets him to explain the problem. A lurid request for sympathy, it's a strange, autobiographical film. Quite why a police-man needs to investigate a suicide isn't explained but hey, that's Ed Wood. The film is affecting, although you're never sure if that's because it's bad or because it's sad.

Poor Bela Lugosi – ruthlessly dropped by Hollywood, he was cast as the sympathetic psychologist, because Wood wanted a name, he wasn't fussy whose, and Lugosi needed a cheque. Lugosi went on to star in four more of Wood's films, most notably *Plan 9 from Outer*

Space, in which he died during the filming and his scenes were finished by a body double: evidently not a good one, as you only ever see him from the back.

An Ed Wood film without at least one angora sweater can only mean that the director himself was wearing it. Even by Hollywood standards Wood was hard to assimilate: he didn't make a statement of his taste for women's clothes, neither did he stay in the closet, he just wore them – prosaically, with a quiet shamelessness and a lack of eroticism. Nonetheless, as *Glen or Glenda* shows, he wasn't entirely at ease with it either.

Growing up in Poughkeepsie, New York, Wood had been dressed as a girl until he was old enough for it to encourage comment. From the age of four or five, Ed Jr showed an interest in film, running around the neighbourhood, often in a dress, taking pictures. Later he began writing screenplays and making films with local kids. He went to movie matinees, and his favourite films were Westerns. Later on, he formed a country & western band.

Wood enlisted in no less a testosterone-packed outfit than the US Marines, six months after Pearl Harbor. Physically big, he won himself a host of medals, lost his front teeth to a rifle butt and took several bullets in the leg, all the while wearing pink underwear under his fatigues (*Nightmare of Ecstasy: The Life and Art of Edward D. Wood Jr,* by Rudolph Grey). In his sexuality, Wood was aggressively het, and no woman in an angora sweater was safe: he had a string of girlfriends, although in 1950s America his x-dressing was to mar some chances of happiness. If nothing else, his girlfriends got fed up with finding their clothes stretched out of shape.

After the War, Ed headed for LA. By 1948, he had chalked up his first failure, a stage-play called *The Casual Company*, also about x-dressing. Only one of Wood's movies, *Bride of the Monster*, ever made any money, and that was after he had sold his rights in it. Wood was driven to write, and compulsively completed screenplays that would never get made. His titles include *Death of a Transvestite* and *Let Me Die in Drag!* The plot of the latter concerned Glen Marker, a TV hit-man on Death Row, who agrees to a taped confession in return for his last wish – to die in drag.

It's possible Wood was a classic heterosexual TV, drawn to become the thing that arouses him. It's equally possible that, after his feminised childhood, it simply made him feel repressed, straitjacketed, half a person, not to wear women's clothes. Whatever the inspiration, it hardly rates as dysfunctional next to his belief that he could make films.

Some Fine Upstanding Transexuals (including TVs)

- Wendy Carlos (b.1939) – American transexual composer and electronic music maker.

- Joan of Arc (1412–1431) – liberated Rheims from the English in the 100 Years' War, in men's clothes.

- Hannah Snell (1723–1792) – dressed as a marine and fought against Bonnie Prince Charlie.

- Pope Paul II (1464–1471) – known to have worn women's clothes and been nicknamed 'Our Lady of Pity'.

- Hatshepsut (1504–1458 BC) – female Pharaoh of ancient Egypt who wore male clothing and a false beard.

- Brandon Teena (1972–1993) – US transexual who was murdered, subject of the film *Boys Don't Cry* (1999).

- Glen Milstead (1945–1988) – actor and drag performer also known as Divine, star of many John Waters films (see pp. 149–51).

- Caroline Cossey (b.1954) – a.k.a. Tula, British transexual *Playboy* model, author and Bond girl in *For Your Eyes Only*.

- RuPaul – a.k.a. RuPaul Andre Charles, American drag queen and television host, who's keen to point out that drag queens don't satirise women: 'I do not impersonate females! How many women do you know who wear seven inch heels, four-foot wigs and skintight dresses?'

- Grayson Perry (b.1960) – ceramicist, whose work sometimes features his shemale alter-ego Claire. Winner of the 2003 Turner Prize for art.

- Candy Darling – TV member of Andy Warhol's Factory, who inspired the Lou Reed songs 'Candy Says' and 'Walk on the Wild Side'.

BETWEEN THE SHEETS – FETISH IN FICTION, PERVERSITY IN VERSE

There have been elements of fetish in literature since Chaucer, while even Arthurian legend is in some ways a sado-masochistic myth. The following writers, however, are singled out for their sensibility. Rather than focusing on erotic writers, defining fetish is a matter of style. There is a noble tradition of autobiographical sex-worker lit, from Xaviera Hollander to Carol Queen and Mistress Chloe, but this section focuses more on works of the imagination. So there's no mention of Anita Philips' finely argued *In Defence of Masochism*, or Susan Sontag's essential essay *On Pornography*.

Fetish takes something darker and more robust than the bohemianism of Henry Miller and Anais Nin, or the swinging group-sex of Catherine M, too. Erotic writing isn't quite the same as fetish writing, because it's theoretically possible to have a novel that is genre fetish fiction without any straight, or 'vanilla', sex at all. Genre fetish fiction began in the 1980s, with novels that owed something to *The Story of O*. Most fetish novels that are meant to arouse have been set in a 'hidden academy' or other context for SM fantasy, while contemporary stories attempt to weave SM plots into more plausible, character-based, everyday tales, which still owe a debt to Sade or Sacher-Masoch.

It now takes a fetish edge to sell erotic books in a space that, in a less explicit age, would have been filled by straighter stories of people bonking. Erotic fiction in the UK used to take its cue from Victorian and Edwardian erotica such as Walter's *My Secret Life*, *A Man with a Maid* or *Maudie*, sometimes by pretending to be the authentic, undiscovered real thing. Buyers used to ask bookshops for 'those books by Anonymous', and this tradition of anonymous authorship continues, for better or worse, in the obviously pseudonymous names of today's fetish fiction writers.

Erotic fiction tries to retain something of an underground, back-street aesthetic even though many bookshops in the UK have sections devoted to it. Americans remain a little more parsimonious, even towards the printed word, and erotica is sometimes to be found, apart from the larger bookstores in sex-positive cities, in the romance section.

But fetish fiction remains, in fact, the last surviving repository of series fiction. Twenty years ago, SF and horror publishing boomed. These days, much of that market has PC gaming, and more competition from other media. Other than series children's fiction, fetish novels are really the last surviving strand of this pulp-fiction approach to publishing.

Going back to the late nineteenth and early twentieth century, French writers such as Louis Aragon and Pierre Louÿs wrote from a semi-fetishistic, fetid pit of imagination, while Britain had its melodramatic, haunting, lyrical strands of fantastical fiction such as that of LeFanu and Wilkie Collins. Today, mainstream fiction occasionally picks up on fetish: either as a literal motif, as in Matthew Branton's crime novel *The House of Whacks*, in which a noir whore heroine is given a SM edge, or in spirit. The literary erotica of Alina Reyes' *The Butcher*, which owes something to the French literary erotic tradition of Marguerite Duras, spills over into finely wrought fetish as the heroine's taste for flesh, butchery and conventionally unappealing old chaps grows.

THE MARQUIS DE SADE (1740–1814)
Sade's surname was appropriated by Kraft-Ebing in his *Psychopathia Sexualis* (1876) to describe the urge to pathological, rampant sexual domination. Brought up as a Bourbon prince, an aristocratic user of the lower orders and a defender of liberty, Sade was a masochist as well as a sadist, indulging himself with prickly switches, a prophylactic stuck with pins and the sodomitic attentions of LaTour, his trusted valet. The tawdry and contradictory

events of Sade's life make him a man of his time. He's been the subject both of censure, a literary Gilles de Rais, and of praise, as one who turned a spotlight on the hypocrisy of the powerful of any regime. Guillaume Apollinaire declared that the writings of the Marquis de Sade would dominate the twentieth century. To Simone de Beauvoir, he was the apotheosis of the misogynistic, pathologically objectifying male; to the surrealists he highlighted the absurdity of the established order. Baudelaire's 'flower of evil', he is the ultimate non-joiner, his body of work a big 'fuck you' to belief in anything other than the irredeemably pathological, primeval nature of the beast within humankind: 'All universal moral principles are idle fantasies.'

And yet, as a moderate revolutionary in the 1790s, he became president of his district of Paris and was imprisoned and sentenced to death for sedition because of his refusal to order executions – only to be released within the year when Robespierre fell. In the mother of all mother-in-law jokes, he spared his own wife's mum from the guillotine, despite the fact that she had been responsible for his imprisonment under the *ancien régime* for over a decade. For all his excesses – and his obesity – he had, it seems, a cad's charm, persuading his wife and mistresses to aid him in the orgiastic lifestyle that got him into so much trouble and was more like a kinky sitcom than Saturnalia.

Unbelievable as it may seem now, Customs and Excise only officially allowed the importation of his works into the UK in 1983. In our dystopic world, where a German cannibal can dispassionately read a Star Trek novel while his consensual victim bleeds to death in the bathroom once they have dined on his penis, Sade's writings seem relevant again, books for kooks indeed.

Sade's most infamous works were written in the 1880s: *Dialogue between a Priest and a Dying Man*, *120 Days of Sodom*, *The Misfortunes of Virtue* and *Aline and Valcour*. We don't get much sense of sweat-sheened skin, of squeals and slaps and sensuality, of gratifying sexual onomatopoeia. There's little of the psychology of submission and domination as it happens in reality. In short, none of the emotional power such extreme situations could have – the Divine Marquis just wasn't an elegant prose stylist. But then he wrote for himself. His writing burns with an advocate's sense of injustice and a pervert's sense of arousal. It was to Sade's own confusion more than anyone's that brutality turned him on. If he'd identified, whenever he sat down to write, whether he was in the mood to write pornography or polemic, he'd have made his legacy a lot less confusing.

The archetypal old perv, if his vices were those of a louche old roué, then so were his sympathies. On the one hand, to be revisionist, Sade was obnoxiously capable of objectifying the lower orders in a way typical of his class and time. On the other, he took huge risks for his own noble notions, turning away from inflicting suffering when it would have maintained his own social rehabilitation.

Not that he wouldn't have got a hard-on to be martyred in any case, but this, together with the series of submissive aristo women whose loyalty he maintained, like some whiskery old dom on the fetish scene, suggests that he just might've known the difference between fantasy and reality after all. A beast-messiah, he's been cited as the worst and best in men. That's why he'll continue to fascinate self-identified pervs and sexual politicians.

LEOPOLD VON SACHER-MASOCH (1836–1895)
Born in to the family of Prague's chief of police, Sacher-Masoch is, in contrast to Sade, the pervert you can read between scenes without ruining your appetite.

Sacher-Masoch himself was an insatiable flagellant. The writings of his wife Wanda spill the beans on the loop-feed of their masochistic relationship, on her enslavement to his need to be enslaved. And she does have a point: keeping a lifestyle slave does involve a lot of unerotic *mise-en-scène* prep work – they're not just for Christmas.

He's best known today thanks to The Velvet Underground's 'Venus in Furs', a paean to the haughty, imperious heroine of Sacher-Masoch's novel of that name, Wanda von Dunajew. The song, like the book, is narrated by Severin, her indentured sex-slave and Sacher-Masoch's thinly veiled alter ego. The novel is not only Sacher-Masoch's best-known work but his most autobiographical, based firmly on a liaison he enjoyed with Fanny Pistor, who appears in the novel as the Baroness Bogdanov.

Most of his tales, like Sade's, feature fabulistic storytelling and broad sweeps of fortune and misfortune, in which vice is rewarded – his heroines lie and cheat their way to wealth and social standing, at least until a payback ending – and virtue never. But there are few similarities beyond that.

Had Kraft-Ebing not coined the term *masochism* along as well as *sadism*, the two would seldom be mentioned in the same breath, other than as fellow members of the canon of pervy literature. Leopold von was in fact horrified to find his name used in this way, and wasn't grateful for being identified as the paradigm of a pathological disorder by the new and as yet unrecognised pseudoscience of psychoanalysis.

Sacher-Masoch is, however, the classic pervert of Freudian case-study: his one-track-minded sexual concerns, which dominated the course of his life, by his own admission stemmed from childhood incidents in which his development had been 'arrested'. Havelock Ellis writes about the time when the young Leopold, hiding behind a dress rail, witnessed his countess aunt's tryst with a lover. On being rumbled, he was taken over her knee and roundly horsewhipped. Later, in his excitement, he heard her apologetic husband being beaten for having discovered the lovers, too.

In *Venus in Furs* Severin chronicles how a fur-clad aunt bound and whipped him until he bled, with an evil smile on her face, then forced him to his knees to thank her for his treatment. 'Under the lash of a beautiful woman my senses first realized the meaning of womanhood. In her fur jacket she seemed to me like a wrathful queen, and from then on my aunt became the most desirable woman on God's earth.'

Sacher-Masoch's women are she-devils made flesh, haughty, statuesque, with a well-turned ankle and a demeanour of the most smouldering contempt. Unlike Sade's parade of broken Coppelias, Sacher-Masoch's women are attractive because of how they think; for the poetry in the cruelty of their sadism. There may be no more tender way to make love than to make your partner tender, but his heroines show no mercy to their captives – they're vituperative, venomous, remorseless sirens who taunt their slaves even until the point of death – a death which serves to confirm their insignificance for them in an irrevocably final and therefore climactic, orgasmic way.

Sacher-Masoch is a broken record if you don't have a taste for his haughty doms, but his evil vixen bitch has become an archetype of fetish culture. There are many formulaic dungeon novels featuring a Machiavellian chatelaine or countess who directs events to increase her number of recalcitrant but strangely attracted slaves. But we can also see his influence, at a pinch, in the vengeful vixens of Eric Stanton's zestful strip cartoons, who, given due cause by some cad, bind, beat and forcibly feminise their way to revenge. Or even in the brutal Varla, Tura Satana's character in Russ Meyer's *Faster, Pussycat! Kill! Kill!*, whose murderous disdain for men is pure Sacher-Masoch heroine turned American gang-girl.

Furs and Fleeces

We may think of them as betokening decadence and amorality today, but in chilly Mitteleurope in the nineteenth century, furs were as everyday a sight as a polar fleece today, as of course were horsewhips. Similarly today, *haute couture* can accommodate overt fetish fashion as much as it likes, but true fetishism remains a private thrill, based firmly on, and continually reinforced by, the everyday. And one perv's everyday (furs and horsewhips) becomes another's exoticism. It does make you wonder if, in a hundred years' time, they'll be paying top dollar for today's polar fleeces, or the dowdy, tweedy numbers of *Catherine M.*

ALGERNON CHARLES SWINBURNE (1837–1909)

Swinburne was a blue-blood through and through. His effete aesthete's outlook was no doubt influenced by his paternal grand-father, who continued to dress as a French nobleman of the *ancien régime* throughout the 1840s. His own father, by contrast, was an upright naval man and his family observed the rituals of High Anglicanism common among its class. On coming down from Oxford, where he always knew his own mind with regard to the many disputes he engaged in, Swinburne associated with the pre-Raphaelites Burne-Jones and Rossetti, and with William Morris. His passion was Italian culture. His other passion was for taking a traditional birching.

His poetry is considered vapid and lightweight today, perhaps, but collections such as *Poems and Ballads* and *A Channel Passage* don't include his works that eulogise flagellation, in which his passion is plain. In the tenor of 'Arthur's Flogging', for example, there are echoes of 'All Things Bright and Beautiful':

> Oh Birch! Thou common dread and doom of all boys,
> Who found out first thy properties of pain
> Who gave thy tough, lithe twigs the power to appal boys?
> Who laid the red foundations of thy reign?

Swinburne was a satirical wind-up merchant, and was fully aware of the harm actual, institutional CP did, too. A sensitive soul, whatever the degree of humiliation and painful punishment he endured during his Eton schooldays, his personal response was to glory in it. It's one survival mechanism, a key to the powerful feelings that submission holds for some. Corporal punishment was seldom written about in the nineteenth century in such sexualised terms as in Swinburne's flagellatory poems, and these were published either anonymously or posthumously.

The adult Swinburne enjoyed the flagellant aspect of his sexuality, while his ambivalence about school discipline is plain in the archness of his satire. In this perhaps he was more thoughtful than the majority of public-school alumni of the time. One can see something of the brutalising hopelessness of real corporal punishment in Swinburne's poem 'Reginald's Flogging', where even an appeal to the supreme authority of the poor lad's father fails to win sympathy. The 'mettle', it seems, that established the British Empire was built not on the playing fields but on the flogging blocks of Eton.

One problem for humanitarians of the time was the difficulty in speaking plainly about the practice. Henry Salt, a reformer, complained that 'One cannot speak in detail on this unpleasant subject.' It follows that not a lot of reform can be achieved without frankness, and Swinburne, in making plain that CP was a powerful source of perverted pleasure, played a part in that debate.

COMTE DE LAUTRÉAMONT (1846–1870)

Unknown during his short life, Lautréamont depicted 'the delights of cruelty' in telling the tale of Maldoror, whose exploits encompass murder, eroticism, sado-masochism, violence, blasphemy and obscenity. The surrealists later adopted him as one of their own. He wrote *Maldoror* while a student in Paris, but had been born Isidore

Lucien Ducasse and raised in Uruguay, the son of a French diplomat, in an atmosphere of civil wars and a grisly cholera epidemic, which must have informed his writing – various animals make their home in Maldoror's rotting body as he still lives.

Under-promoted by skittish publishers for years, it wasn't until the 1927 publication of *Lautréamont at Any Cost* by surrealists Philippe Soupault and André Breton that Lautréamont found a permanent place in French literature. During his lifetime, according to his publisher, Lautréamont 'only wrote at night seated at his piano. He would declaim his sentences as he forged them, punctuating his harangues with chords.'

OCTAVE MIRBEAU (1848–1917)

The Torture Garden, first published in 1898, is probably known to most people today as the novel which has lent its name to London's thriving fetish club, but it's far more than pornographic in intent. Often seen as a disciple of Sade, Mirbeau was also far more than a pornographer but, like Sade, he walked the line where perversion met political theory – and walked it much straighter. A successful author, he was, if you like, a champagne anarchist, known in his own lifetime – inaccurately, given the black of the anarchist flag – as 'the red millionaire'. All of Mirbeau's work is concerned with the hypocrisies of everyday life, with the idea that there is no such thing as the use of power, only its abuse.

Although far more than a disciple of Sade, and in fact a far better writer, he took the latter's dystopic views to a more crystallised, clarified extreme in which all human endeavour is seen as murderous in intent. It's a logical extreme not only of Sade but of the ethics of Baudelaire's *Flowers of Evil*, and *The Torture Garden* remains his best expression of his position. Sade is always open to criticism over the issue that all his sexual concerns are male dom/fem sub, but Mirbeau runs the gamut. 'Blood,' says Clara in *The Torture Garden*, 'is the wine of love.'

Mirbeau dives effortlessly to a level of cynicism that other writers would shrink from, and swimming in his literary waters presents a wonderfully clear vision of evil. It's not so much a question of Sade's 'beast in man', but the observation that humans are no more than beasts anyway. The established order in all its spheres is based on usury, extortion and the great protection racket that is government. In the words of Woody Guthrie, 'Some rob you with a six-gun, and some with a fountain pen.'

Moral distinctions do not exist in Mirbeau's world: there are only cruelty, power, dominion, lust, slavery, submission, sickness and beauty. The garden of the novel's title is a vast collection of plants, flowers, trees and animals that the Chinese government has constructed and maintained in perfect equilibrium. In the centre of this lush, fantastic and deliriously beautiful landscape exists a field of torture and execution where all the most painful, ingenious and malevolent devices of cruelty ever invented reside. The flowers are washed with blood, the soil is tilled with the remains of corpses created by the pits of torture, and in this garden thousands of 'useless' citizens are made to feel the direst extremities of suffering.

In the garden, torture goes hand-in-hand with the cultivation of life. Flowers are grown upon the gallows themselves. Corpses nourish the soil. Mirbeau makes it very clear that the garden is supposed to be a symbol of the world, and that the threads of beauty, pain, suffering and pleasure that the world holds for us are so finely intertwined that we cannot separate them. The tortures in the garden are so fiendish that, as their victims' lives ebb away, Mirbeau is daring us to be titillated, pornographically, as if to say, 'See, this element of titillation is the very source of human ingenuity and cruelty.'

Mirbeau, in contrast to Sade, has no chip on his shoulder. There is no 'look at me' quality to his writing – he is the writer as observer.

His authorial voice is anonymous; he is a spy, not a participant, in the house of hate, because that's how you get a better observational job done. For a disciplined writer, an ego like Sade's only interferes. Mirbeau's work is crystalline, utterly unconcerned with self-justification, and all the more powerful for it. He was too much of a worldly man to be possessed of an idealism that could be anything other than thwarted, and his work is both pornography and a sincere attempt to make sense of a difficult world. Mirbeau allows the reader to find arousal in suffering, because, if the reader finds sexual gratification in his work, it only proves his point. As does the fact that his work has consistently been marketed throughout its publishing history as erotica. Mirbeau is probably the best example of Angela Carter's notion of a moral pornographer.

GEORGES BATAILLE (1897–1962)
French surrealist writer, academic and mild-mannered transgressive, most famous for *Story of the Eye* (1928), Bataille put a new and brutal spin on the long tradition of French anti-clerical fiction. He had been tempted by the priesthood and went to a Catholic seminary. When he lost his faith in the 1920s, he put as much devotion into his faithlessness. A nihilistic, Bonnie-and-Clyde story of priest-killing, his most famous novel is a hefty kick in the eye for an institution whose gaze has oppressed as much as its grace has helped. A contributor to many journals, he wasn't well-known in his lifetime, but Foucault and Derrida both acknowledged a big debt.

PAULINE RÉAGE (1907–1998)
Pauline Réage was not the first but the second professional pseudonym of Anne Desclos, a tweedy, intellectual scholar, translator and publisher who, as Dominique Aury, translated many works of English literature – by Swinburne, Woolf, Waugh, Eliot and Scott Fitzgerald – into French, and introduced many readers to their

writing with her accessible criticism, as well as sitting on the judicial panels of leading French literary prizes. But her anonymity as the author, too, of the famous SM novel *The Story of O* has done nothing to hurt its sales.

Published in 1954, *O* is a single-minded, focused fantasy of female submission in which a Parisian fashion photographer is blindfolded, chained, whipped, masked and trained to be constantly available for anyone who desires her. It chronicles a journey towards complete sexual objectification and personal fulfilment, until for O time itself is no longer her own. In fantasy, of course, everything that is done to you feels just the way you want it to. Aury was a high-achiever and there's no contradiction here. This is sophisticated sexual unreality, not some Gorean manifesto (see p. 173) for the good life.

After graduating from the Sorbonne and working as a journalist, Aury joined the publishers Gallimard, where her lover and boss (smart girl) made the chauvinistic remark that a woman couldn't write a decent erotic novel. Aury set out to prove him wrong and so, ironically, this blueprint for female sexual submission was conceived as a feisty, blue-stockinged response to a male assumption.

The heroine of the novel has the shortest possible name, reduced to one letter, a label – just a number, but a bit more poetic. Critical speculation encompassed not just Réage's identity but what 'O' could stand for, some suggesting *object* or *orifice*, but it is in fact an abbreviation of the name Odile. Aury's point remained privately proved to her lover, and that's the way she wanted it. Many disputed that the author was a woman, and in that climate few would have believed it was the demure, intellectual and almost prudish Aury. In addition, the book attracted controversy: obscenity charges were dismissed in 1959 but resulted in a ban on publicity, although not sale, that wasn't lifted in France until 1967. In an interview with the *New Yorker* in 1975, forty years after it was first written and in a different sexual climate, Aury finally came out as Réage.

L'histoire d'O has supplied a formula for female-submissive sex writing ever since, much of it by women writers who are more self-identified and 'sex-positive' than Aury was. The Susie Bright approach would have probably rankled with her European sense of finesse. The book had been written to prove a private point, with something of the sex-war wit of Dorothy Parker and her chums at the Algonquin Hotel. In so doing, Aury also provided a model for respectable anonymity in sex writing that has inspired the likes of Catherine M. It's always the quiet ones.

PHILIP LARKIN (1922–1985)

This favourite of post-war British poetry was posthumously revealed to be Britain's spanking laureate. The lonely, egg-headed, bicycling Hull librarian had a penchant for giving hand-spankings, and an enviable collection of spanking magazines. Perhaps this isn't surprising, considering the steady, loose but precise metre of his poetry. In contrast to his poignant, disappointed poetry, Larkin wrote two private-school flagellation novels that betray an expectedly fine if unsubtle sense of erotic humiliation. Extending his love of jazz even to his dark side, Larkin toyed with a pseudonym, Brunette Coleman.

Larkin understood the genre. While he was poignantly disappointed by his lack of success in mainstream fiction, he clearly relished pastiching the schoolgirl literature in which he was steeped: Brunette's books are titled *Trouble at Willow Gables* and *Michaelmas Term at St Bride's*.

All the elements of a perverted story are there: uniforms; details of the buttocks of schoolgirls, especially slightly plump ones; matron-supervised bladder and bowel control; beatings from the headmistress. In one scene a heroine gets lost in the woods at night, tears the seat of her tight trousers and has to spend the morning with her bum bare. Larkin winks at the reader though terribly English and red-faced. They fuck you up, your mum and dad, indeed.

YUKIO MISHIMA (1925–1970)

'Live briefly but gloriously. One's evanescent life is but a preparation for death. The fall of the blossom is as moving as its beauty on the limb and the final moment, as ceremonialized in the ritual of seppuku, is indeed the moment of truth.' *Hari-Kiri* (Jack Seward, 1968)

At the height of his career, after having achieved international fame and literary notoriety, Yukio Mishima committed ritual suicide. At the age of 45, he performed the Japanese rite known as *seppuku*, which begins with disembowelling and ends – if possible – with decapitation, and ordinarily requires a minimum of two participants.

On 25 November 1970, Mishima and members of the Tatenokai (the Shield Society, Mishima's own small private army) took over the headquarters of the Japanese Self-Defence Force (the non-offensive army that was allowed for by Japan's post-war constitution). After failing to make the squaddies listen to his speech, Mishima plunged a ritual sword into his stomach. One of his followers died with him.

Many reasons have been advanced for his suicide, and many of them are political: a final tribute to the samurai spirit; an infatuation with death and night and blood; a desire for immortality; a protest against Japan's General MacArthur-inspired constitution. In the West, we understand a public suicide best as a protest of some kind, informed by a messianic religious tradition. Others, more correctly, identify the sexual motive of his death. To Mishima, its public nature did not necessarily mean he was making a statement. It's quite possible he was simply compelled to have the experience of a public death.

Over a highly productive lifetime, Mishima published over twenty novels and a host of short stories, dramas and one-act plays. His best-known works include *Confessions of a Mask, The Temple of the Golden Pavilion, The Sound of Waves, Spring Snow* and *After the Banquet*. Sickly as a boy, Mishima conditioned and strengthened his body with the daily practice of kendo and karate. In an interview he commented that he worked hard on his body because he intended to die before he was fifty, and wanted to make sure he had a good-looking corpse. Mishima's prose is beautiful, and he is a complex man. His homosexuality and his fetish of the military gave him a sense of a transgressive, socially disapproved-of inner life, which could be expressed through conservative means and seem all the more straight-backed for it.

Like Wilde, whom he admired, Mishima was married, but unlike Wilde he wasn't in the least bisexual. In *Confessions of a Mask*, the mask is a reference to an outward identity necessary for existence in a homophobic, rigid society. But a mask was also a theatrical means of expression, especially in Japan. Mishima's Tatenokai were intended to be a protective force for the Japanese Emperor, based on samurai codes and similar to the Roman Praetorian Guard or Saddam Hussein's *Fedayeen*, something he claimed was constitutionally lacking in the new Japan. In reality, there was a strong sexual compulsion to the creation of Mishima's toy soldiers: 'The soldiers' odour of sweat ... struck my nostrils and intoxicated me ... It did gradually and tenaciously arouse within me a sensuous craving for such things as the destiny of soldiers, the tragic nature of their calling, the distant countries they would see, the ways they would die' (*Confessions of a Mask*).

Mishima is thought of as a social conservative, someone who found the influence of the West pernicious. But he had many Western friends, admired Western art and, like Jean Genet, Jean Cocteau and Sade, thought that life was a brutal game against hard odds. Perhaps it's fair to say that he liked the West but felt it belonged there. His Tatenokai are usually seen as an expression of his political beliefs, but that's not to take account of his fetishistic sexuality. His life is confusing when we look for some kind of high-minded explanation for actions like the establishment of a private army, and a public suicide, and discount sexuality from such statesman-like concerns. But Mishima would have identified with Nietzsche – 'a person's sexuality reaches to the summit of their soul' – and considered his sexuality high-minded. His explanation is there in his writings, which contain presentiments of early death that are spooky to read – one realises he had been driven towards something at least like the manner of his death for years beforehand.

From his earliest days, Mishima was drawn to morbid, necrophilic images such as he found in a poem by Wilde: *Fair is the knight who lieth slain/Amid the rush and reed . . .* In his work he speaks of the 'cold grace in which life and death coexist'. He viewed life as an arrow's arc and wanted to control the trajectory of his own to the end. Mishima was a loon, but his social eccentricities were seen in the context of his being a prolific writer and, as it were, a ramrod-straight citizen. His violent, self-harming paraphilia – to become like his lust-objects; to become dead – was understood in a context which allowed it to continue unchecked, until the legend of death and night and blood overshadows the finesse of his writing.

J.G. BALLARD (b. 1930)

James Graham Ballard is known for the remarkable range of his novels: from science fiction to autobiographical history to novels of British manners. All are unmistakably Ballard, whatever the genre, and deal in dystopias with a uniquely British brand of surrealism. Ballard captures a sense of unreality about his own life – from his bizarre childhood as a captive of the Japanese during World War II to the accidental death of his wife – and those of his characters.

Ballard's writing has always moved with the times, while remaining challenging and outside them. He has enjoyed particular success with *Empire of the Sun* and, more recently, *Cocaine Nights* and *Super-Cannes*, but here it's worth mentioning *Crash*, part of the 'Dystopian Trilogy' along with *High-Rise* and *Concrete Island*, and his most fetishistic work, which has achieved global cult status and was filmed faithfully by David Cronenberg.

The one aspect of *Crash* that Cronenberg's film understandably forgoes is its Englishness: it is specific to the world of sprawling West London, the dormitory commuter areas around the A40. Ballard captures a soulless environment where beauty has been sacrificed to the car. *Crash* is an intensely moral work: its hero and heroine are able to develop their intensely sexual fetish of cars, twisted metal, flesh and wrecks because other sources of aesthetic pleasure have been removed. At the start of the novel, the hero has an elevated motorway right outside his apartment: Ballard portrays fetishism as a coping mechanism, a means of adaptation to a hostile world. As they grow more obsessive, his characters recreate car accidents of the famous, indulge in near-death automotive games and are turned on by the medical accessories of car-crash victims. Like another Ballard novel which has SM sex in it, *Atrocity Exhibition*, this isn't an erotic novel: Ballard describes an obsessive, inexorably deadly fetishism, in which driving becomes more sexually compelling than sex.

JOHN NORMAN (b. 1931)

A controversial, reactionary philosopher and utopian science fiction novelist, Norman is best known for his *Chronicles of Gor*. A philosophy professor at the City University of New York, he is a

complex if misguided man, similar to Ayn Rand in having controversial attitudes that alienate politically correct literary elites and
yet attract a grassroots following. Norman's fans are called Goreans,
and thrive on the internet. They believe in the remedial power of a
natural order, a Nietzschean hierarchy of talents, in which men will
naturally show themselves superior to women. His novels are
manifestos of female submission that are best described as erotic
SF. They sold well during the 1960s and 1970s, when Americans
were more inclined to explore alternative societies through utopian
SF by writers such as Robert Heinlein.

The extent to which Norman himself is a Gorean is unclear,
although his politics moved from conservative to libertarian during
a period of what he considered undeclared censorship within
publishing and the SF community. Considered by Goreans to be
not a misogynist but a sexual pioneer, Norman divides people. The
world of Gore is an irony-free zone compared to the playful world
of 'carnivalesque', involving switching or ritual spirituality, that
most European SMers see themselves as part of. (If you believe that
SM practice is a literal-minded manifesto for real life, then how are
you ever going to 'become other'?) His 1974 non-fiction book
Imaginative Sex is well thought of, emphasises the consensual and
is introduced by Pat Califa. However, many people feel that
Goreans should get a (real) life.

ANGELA CARTER (1940–1992)

'Their pleasure was pure because it was so restrained.'

As a child, Angela Carter was evacuated from London to stay with
her grandmother in Yorkshire. One imagines an old woman spark-
ing the young girl's interest in fairytales, weaving compelling
versions that inspired Carter's collection of feminist fairytales *The
Bloody Chamber*, in which she took on the role of Mother Goose,
with versions of 'Alice in Wonderland', 'Little Red Riding Hood'

and 'Bluebeard' among others, that bring out the sexual and sado-masochistic subtexts of these timeless stories.

Carter's work refers to Chaucer, Shakespeare, Lawrence, Wordsworth and Coleridge, Blake, Mansfield, Woolf, Dickens, Keats, Bram Stoker and Lewis Carroll … and many, many more. She spoke French and German and wrote extensively on Sade, informed by Bataille, Luce Irigaray and de Beauvoir. *The Sadeian Woman* (1978) is her non-fiction examination of his pornography, and she evolves a notion of moral pornography that is both arousing and a critique of sexual relations. Carter compares fantasy and reality in Sade's broken heroine Justine, but concludes that pro- and anti-porn arguments are missing the point, in not focusing on the quality of the pornographic experience. Carter continued her dream-like, fetishistic magic realism in *Nights at the Circus* (1984). In the circus, fairground and music hall, she describes a world in which all terror and anxiety is forgotten in a haze of greasepaint and smoke, yet their dramas spell out the realities of the audience's lives.

The Infernal Desire Machine of Doctor Hoffman (1972) was her first publication, and in these short stories she showcases the fetishistic overtones that run throughout her many novels, such as *Nothing Sacred* (1982) and *Wise Children* (1991). In *Love* (1992), she asks, 'In a relationship, where does one being end and the other begin, what happens to the individuals who become codependent?' Love is not the romantic image we have but, often, a cruel and injurious arena in which there are no victors.

She was also greatly influenced by a two-year stay in Japan in the 1970s, having won the Somerset Maugham prize for Literature. She remarked that Maugham would have been pleased to know that she used the £500 prize money – which went further back then – to run away from British culture. As Margaret Attwood observed, she revelled in the diverse. She revelled also in the perverse and the fantastical, and was a minx with her prose, playing games with the reader.

ANNE RICE (b. 1941)

Anne Rice's horror and fantasy novels have been bestsellers since the 1970s. Most famous for her Vampire Chronicles, *Interview with the Vampire*, *The Vampire L'Estat* and *Queen of the Damned*, as well as stories about mummies and witches, she has spent her life in New Orleans, where most of her novels are set. Her books are lyrical cornerstones of goth subculture, reaching evocatively throughout history to follow the different lives of her immortal and mildly homoerotic characters. Rice has also written SM erotica as Anne Rampling (notably *Exit to Eden*) and A. N. Roquelaire (*The Claiming of Sleeping Beauty* trilogy). Used to finding daily crowds of fans at her door, she has recently moved to a gated community within New Orleans.

CYBERPUNK (b.1984)

'Twenty years past 1984, how free do *you* feel?' Bruce Sterling

Cyberpunk is the antithesis of *Star Trek*. In the 1980s, far from exploring strange new frontiers, SF went west. Since the 1960s, SF had explored sexuality as part of its Utopian tradition: novels of alternative societies presented worlds with different mores to our own. The 1970s had been its boom years, and *Playboy* had been a popular outlet for innovative SF short stories. Books by writers such as Ursula Le Guin, Philip Jose Farmer, Robert Heinlein, Sheri S. Tepper and Brian Aldiss featured themes such as female-dominated societies, single-sex societies or worlds whose inhabitants could change sex at will. In response to the growth of feminism and the social experiments of the 1960s, writers created imaginary worlds in which they could play out or mythologise alternative models to our own society. Cecilia Tan, meanwhile, cut to the chase with imaginative SF erotica, while otherwise the most fetishistic of fantastical SF series must be Frank Herbert's *Dune* trilogy, in which the political machinations and the differing aptitudes of the houses of Atreides and Harkonnen are carried out with a measured sadism worthy of imperial Rome or mediaeval Venice.

In the 1980s, however, utopian SF became dystopian SF: where SF social structures had been impenetrable, glacial, efficient governing machines, now they reflected our own concerns about global power and its abuse, and featured the power dynamics between corrupt semi-corporate governments and those subject to them. The book that set the tone for cyberpunk was William Gibson's *Neuromancer* (1984). Similar writers include Bruce Sterling and Michael Swanwick. 'Cyberpunk' is a conjunction of 'cyber', because computers are enmeshed into the very fabric of these societies, and 'punk', because the genre featured a return to fiction's formal elements, away from the progressive speculations of utopian SF, returning to the detective plots of pulp crime stories – the fictional equivalent of a satisfying three-chord thrash.

Cyberpunk novels are often thought of as nihilistic but that isn't really the case – the human spirit-jewel of resistance and survival is usually visible amid its grinding cyber-industrial complexes. Old-school SF, meanwhile, was busily transmuting itself into Tolkienesque fantasy, with immense commercial success for a few, or 'hard' SF – fiction with the emphasis on science where loving ten-page descriptions of particle accelerators are not uncommon.

Cyberpunk takes a fetishistic attitude to the body. Like Philip Marlowe, its heroes are invariably sexually frustrated, while their lives intertwine with those of heroines who are part Lara Croft and

Tank-Girl-tomboy, and part Lana Turner. Political correctness replaces 1940s morality as a source of sexual tension. Helpmeet/Amazon replaces Madonna/whore as the paradoxical fulcrum of female behaviour. By the time of *The Matrix* – hugely cyberpunk in influence – Trinity is a real Mary Magdalene, getting her hands dirty by day (albeit with killing instead of paid sex) and being a supportive, empowering lover to her messianic chap come the evening. Meanwhile, the boundaries of the body are broken down, just like the borders of nation-states. This is not through sexual predation but commercial technology. In many stories, the action takes place in a virtual world, created by neural connections and pathways along which human becomes machine and vice versa, as in the *Matrix* films and Cronenberg's *exiStenZ*. These superhighways are two-way streets: both sources of dangerous oppression for the human mind and opportunities to explore without physical travel.

The theme of broken-down physical boundaries is similar to the sensibility of body modification. Cyberpunk asks us to picture a web of neural, surgical connections and bio-mechanics: plug-ins which turn us into either slaves or supermen, either restricting and disciplining us or amplifying our actions. Accessing the virtual world is often a ritualised process in which the human body goes on standby. Stories which reflect anti-globalisation and ecological themes also helped to make cyberpunk a 1990s phenomenon.

Ridley Scott's film *Bladerunner* was based on cyberpunk-inspiration Philip K. Dick's short story *Do Androids Dream of Electric Sheep?* It influenced the idea of commercial, dystopic worlds, seen also in *Minority Report*. Popularly, cybersex was a concept with common currency in which seated, suited, gloved participants could have virtual-reality congress like video-conferencing. There's little VR sex in actual fiction, though. The real legacy of cyberpunk is in computer gaming and fashion; in our attitude to the internet and in informing the dot-com boom; in Trinity's rubber suit in *The Matrix*, and Margaret Attwood's marvellous dystopias.

SLASH FICTION

Slash fiction is an evolutionary twist in literary history. For copyright reasons it is illegal, conventionally unpublishable and often carried out under pseudonyms. Though it began in SF magazines in the mid-1970s, it owes its growth to the internet. Slash fiction takes popular characters from SF and gives them a sexuality. Purists define its subject-matter as exclusively gay male, and it is usually written by women.

The phenomenon takes its name from the '/' symbol, as early stories were named simply after the characters they featured: male 'buddy' pairings such as 'Spock/McCoy'. *Star Trek* was the basis of the majority of stories; particularly Kirk, Spock and the cultural confusions of Vulcan sexuality, such as Spock's 'amok time'. More down-home slash experiments have included Bodie/Doyle and Starsky/Hutch. Of course it doesn't take a genius to see the satirical possibilities of slash, beyond SF – there's even a John Wayne slash-style website – which suggest it will remain a genuinely transgressive phenomenon.

CELEBRITY SPANKING

Well, we've come to the end of this eclectic collection of all things fetish. Of course, we haven't been able to provide an exhaustive, definitive list, and if your favourite fetish icon is missing from *Fetish Facts*, then sorry, but be assured this is due to limitations of space, rather than ignorance of their existence. Before we call it a wrap, there is just enough time to mention kinky capers in the public eye. Classically, as we all know, a kinky past can come back to spank a celeb on the bum. In 2004, this happened to one of three finalists in *Joe Millionaire*, a US reality TV show in which a bevy of America's finest competed for the affections of a man they believed to be a relaxed, handsome millionaire, who was, in fact, a penniless builder. While Fox TV described blonde Sarah Kozer's occupation as 'sales and design', the Smoking Gun website turned up a clutch of playful bondage films such as *Novices in Knots, Hogtied* and *Helpless Heroines*, as well as foot-fetish fare such as *Dirty Soled Dolls*, in which she plays a smiling, starring role. She's blindfolded, gagged and bound in all manner of elaborate rope or duct-tape bondage, tickled and spanked, sometimes in her woolly street clothes (including one sweater in which she also posed for her Fox publicity photo), also as a cheerleader and nurse. There's even some elaborate toe-bondage. Ironically, one film features Kozer and a male co-star as contestants on a spoof TV show offering a $1m prize, in which both contestants are bound and gagged and race to free themselves, and which opens with a scrawl reading 'Reality television has hit a new low.' Poor lass.

But Madonna, by contrast, is hardly the only famous woman to have flirted willingly in the media with pervy fun. In the cat-spat for column inches, showing a bit of cheek here and there doesn't do any harm. Here's a top twelve of shiny happy women who've had a positive spin from the tabloids:

1. Liz Hurley: The model and actress made an admission which was reported in the newspapers that her favourite party game is having to bend over and let different people smack her behind and guessing who it is. Also, a newspaper article about a relationship between Liz and movie producer William Annesley mentions that he told a group of businessmen, 'We liked a bit of spanking. Elizabeth liked to spank me, then have me spank her. Spanking is an English public school thing, I suppose. Nothing vicious, just a hand or the back of a hairbrush on the bare bottom.'

2. Angelina Jolie: The *Lara Croft* actor, refugee campaigner and all-round good egg spoke routinely of her dark and kinky pleasures with horn-dog husband Billy Bob Thornton. Sadly, as a friend of hers said of their marriage, 'She agreed to kinky bedroom games, but it was never enough.' In 2002, Angie demanded that Billy Bob return five phials of her blood, which she had exchanged with him in a blood-letting sex ritual, fearing he would use them to put a curse on her.

3. Tracy Shaw: The actress voted Britain's sexiest soap star in 2001 dressed in a school uniform with a group of friends at a party. That was it, but Tracy did feel the slipper at least once during her schooldays.

4. Jordan: In an article in the *Sun* in 2004, the model's former partner Warren Furman (a.k.a. Ace from top TV show *Gladiators*) said that Jordan would beg him to spank her and use a bullwhip on her. He added, 'She complained that I didn't spank her hard enough – she said the pain it gave her turned her on.'

5. Britney Spears: According to an article on an internet website, the American singer played along humorously when a Hollywood shopkeeper said he was going to spank her for causing noise and disruption in his shop.

6. Catherine Zeta Jones: To publicise her appearance on the VH1 show *Ten of the Best*, where different celebrities come on each week to pick their ten favourite songs, the Welsh actress was photographed looking stern and bending a school cane.

7. Jenny McCarthy: The American model and actress presented the 1998 MTV Europe music awards. Introducing Aqua, she said, 'The band we're about to see next are so damn perky I wanna put 'em across my lap and spank 'em.' Jenny also administered a swat of the paddle to three fraternity pledges on TV, and she told them to 'Thank sister Jenny for each one.'

8. Joanna Lumley: In an interview in the *Sunday Telegraph*, the British actress acutely observed the difference between fantasy and reality. 'Men don't mind being spanked by women, but they don't want to be led by them.'

9. Davina McCall: The saucy British TV presenter holidayed in the south of France with her boyfriend, the footballer Stan Collymore. As they topped up their tans, Collymore jokingly tried on her bikini top and the couple spanked each other on the backside with a bat. At the 2000 Q magazine music awards she arrived to present them brandishing a riding crop. Collymore, meanwhile, was suspended from his job at BBC Radio Five over revelations that he was a fan of the hobby of dogging. If he turns up on time, with his tie straight, and gives good commentary, should we care?

10. Emma Bunton: To publicise the launch of a 2001 single, the artist formerly known as Baby Spice appeared at a party, pictured in the *Sun* and the *Daily Mail*, dressed as a schoolmistress and twirling a cane. Bunton was quoted as saying, 'I always wanted to be a schoolteacher and teach well-behaved children.' Asked if she was well-behaved at school she replied, 'There was one unfortunate incident when I let off a fire extinguisher.' She didn't comment on the measures subsequently taken.

11. Geri Halliwell: As well as posing with the prizes on a Spanish game show, Geri once modelled a picture that was used on an edition of the erotic classic *A Man with a Maid*, wearing Edwardian bloomers and holding an apple. The former Spice Girl and erstwhile United Nations representative once said in a newspaper interview, 'I'd love to spank every member of Parliament – and be a headmistress!' A picture with the article showed Geri dressed as a schoolgirl holding a cane.

12. Davinia Taylor: On the Sky One programme *50 Ways to Tease Your Lover*, the British actress said she went for a schooldays theme for turning her lover on, including dressing as a schoolgirl, and as a headmistress who can 'give him the cane'. How British.

Speaking of Liz Hurley, Viyella-shirted former paramour and airbrushed Hollywood heartthrob Hugh Grant has a couple of on-screen brushes with fetish, one of which he might rather forget. First, he appeared in Ken Russell's *Lair of the White Worm* (from the Bram Stoker novella) playing a rather hapless hero like a rabbit caught in headlights. The film is fairly execrable but does nonetheless feature Amanda Donohoe in a rubber suit. Secondly, he played the stiff, reserved and freaked-out Englishman to perfection in Polanski's fetid *Bitter Moon* – a foil for the story of the obsessional lovers he and his wife are travelling with, who so exhaust their pervy passions that not even grunting around in animal masks can raise their interest any longer.